Thomas Fry

A New System of Finance

proving the defects of the present system, that a saving may take place in the public income and expenditure to the amount of near ten millions annually

Thomas Fry

A New System of Finance

proving the defects of the present system, that a saving may take place in the public income and expenditure to the amount of near ten millions annually

ISBN/EAN: 9783337287450

Printed in Europe, USA, Canada, Australia, Japan

Cover: Foto ©Suzi / pixelio.de

More available books at **www.hansebooks.com**

A NEW SYSTEM OF FINANCE:

PROVING

The Defects of the Present System;

That a Saving may take place in the Public Income and Expenditure to the Amount of near Ten Millions annually!

Exposition of the Consequences to the Public through their Connection with the Bank of England;

The baneful Consequence of Stock-jobbing;

Astonishing Losses sustained by the Public, that have enabled the Minister to carry on the Deception of lessening the Public Debt;

The unparalleled Advantages given by the Minister to the Loan Mongers for Paper Credit, in order to support the present ruinous War;

One Hundred Pounds Securities in the Three per Cents. given by the Minister to receive 4 l. 10 s. 8 d. to be sent to Germany for the Support of the Emperor's Loan.

Together with a REPLY to Messrs. MORGAN and VANSITTART on the Subject of Finance.

Some Remarks on Simon the Stock Broker's Letter to Mr. Alderman Curtis, late Lord Mayor of London.

On the Iniquity of Private Tontines.

Schemes for the Benefit of Age, on the most reputable Establishments.

A reasonable Compromise between Debtor and Creditor.

A perfect Establishment for National Credit in future;

And THE PEOPLE RELIEVED FROM THE MOST BURTHENSOME OF THEIR TAXES.

By *THOMAS FRY*,
AUTHOR OF THE GUARDIAN OF PUBLIC CREDIT.

LONDON:

PRINTED FOR THE AUTHOR;
And sold by J. S. JORDAN, No. 166, Fleet-street; and C. CHAPPEL, No. 66, Pall Mall.

M DCC XCVII.

AN EXPOSITION, &c.

THE present alarming state of public credit, the consequent failures of houses of the first respectability, in a word, the ruin upon which the nation is verging—while the authors of the public afflictions and dangers are pursuing their career, and wallowing in the wealth acquired by sacrifices which they have made of the constitutional freedom of the British empire—cannot be too ardently urged, nor too minutely enquired into, by every man who wishes to maintain the least pretensions to public virtue, or regard for the national prosperity.

Private interest, it has been lately asserted, obtains that predominant regard, which, in former times, Englishmen bestowed on liberty alone. Certain recent laws, perhaps, establish the fact; but it is left to him who preserves the ancient spirit of the country to offer such information as may open men's eyes to their pecuniary interest, since every other principle holds a subordinate place.

The funding system may be considered as the fountain from which the extravagant and sanguinary wars that have for a century disgraced this country, derive their strength and nourishment; wars that have impeded the course of national happiness—which, instead of contracting, would have increased and extended with the natural progress of manufactures, trade, and refinement.

Though I have given my opinion refpecting the contract between peace and war, numbers may differ from me refpecting the neceffity of it; but when I claim juftice for the public debtor of a nation as well as the public creditor, (which is the intention of this work) with all fenfible and honeft men I am certain I cannot have a fingle negative. It is a conduct that hath been reverfed in this country ever fince the commencement of funding in order to raife fupplies for the public expenditure, but at no former period fo wickedly extravagant as in that of the prefent adminiftration. I therefore now find myfelf under the neceffity of producing the facts that will prove my affertions in this important bufinefs; and as I have no party to fupport, fhall candidly ftate the progreffive conduct of the different adminiftrations refpecting finance from the year 1745 down to the prefent time. The particulars are taken from the Commiffioners' Accounts, ftating the publick income and expenditure, publifhed by authority of Parliament, 21ft of March, 1786.

Abftract of Appendix No. 1, page 70.
"MEMORANDUM.

"The fubfcribers of 100l. to the lottery 1745 were allowed an annuity for one life of 9s a ticket, which amounted to 22,500l. but is now reduced by lives falling in to 12,383l. 12s.;—and the fubfcribers of 100l. to the lottery 1746 were allowed an annuity for one life of 18s. a ticket, which amounted to the fum of 45,000l. but is now reduced by lives falling in to 22,82ıl. 10s.;—and the fubfcribers for 100l. to the 3l. per Cent. Annuities 1757, were allowed an annuity for one life on 1l. 2s. 6d. which amounted to the fum of 33,750l. but is now reduced by lives falling in to 25,213l. 7s. 6d.;—and the fubfcribers for 100l. to the 3l. per Cent. Annuities 1761, were allowed an annuity for 99 years for every 100l. of 1l. 2s. 6d. amounting with charges of management to the Bank of of England, to 130,053l. 10s. 3d.;—and the fubfcribers of 12,000,000l. for the fervice of the year 1762 were intituled to an annuity of 1l. per cent. for 98 years, which, with charges of management to the Bank of England, amounted to 121,687l. 10s. which annuities for 98 and 99 years were confolidated by act of 4th Geo. II. 3 R. S;—and the fubfcribers of 5,000,000l. for the fervice of the year 1777, were allowed an annuity of 10s. for every 100l. contributed, for 10 years, from the 5th of April 1777, which amounted, with charges of management to the Bank of England, to 25,351l. 11s. 3d;—and the fubfcribers for 6,000,000l. for the year 1778, were allowed an annuity of 2l. 10s. for every 100l. contributed, for thirty years, from the 5th of January 1778, which amounted, with charges of management to the Bank of England, to 152,069l. 6s. part of which fum hath been by the fubfcribers changed for life annuities, amounting to the fum of 2849l. 13s. but is now reduced by lives falling in to the fum of 2769l. 13s;—and the fubfcribers of 7,000,000l. for the fervice of the year 1779, were allowed an annuity of 3l. 15s. for every 100l. contributed, for 29 years, from the 5th day of January 1779, or for life, which with charges of management to the Bank of England, amounted to 266,116l. 12s. 2d. part of which fum hath been by the fubfcribers changed for life annuities, amounting to the fum of 5,318l. 18s. 7d;—and the fubfcribers of 12,000,000l. for the fervice of the year 1780, were allowed an annuity of 1l. 16s. 3d. for every 100l. contributed, for eighty years, from the 5th day of January 1780, which amounted, with charges of management to the Bank of England, to the fum of 220,558l. 11s. 10d;—and the fubfcribers of 13,500,000l. for the fervice of the year 1782, were allowed an annuity of 17s. 6d. for every 100l. contributed, for 78 years, from the 5th of January 1782, which amounted, with charges of management to the

Bank of England, to the sum of 119,786l. 2s. 9d;—and the subscribers of 12,000,000l. for the year 1783, were allowed an annuity of 13s. 4d. for every 100l. contributed, for 77 years, from the 5th of January 1783, which amounted, with charges of management to the Bank of England, to the sum of 81,125l;—and the subscribers of 6,000,000l. for the service of the year 1784, were allowed an annuity of 5s. 6d. for every 100l. contributed, for 75 years and six months, from the 5th of July 1784, which amounted, with charges of management to the Bank of England, to the sum of 16,732l. 16s. 7d$\frac{1}{2}$. All which annuities are an increase to the annual interest, but cannot be added to the national debt, as no money was advanced for the same."

These are the express words of the Committee for liquidating the accounts for the year 1786.

This makes a total in annuities of 1,193,674l. 7s. 3d.

which sum in itself contracted, for which no more was received, would have been more than sufficient to have discharged the whole of the debt, prior to Mr. Pitt's funding.

The following extract is separated with a view of rendering more apparent the particular charge of management by the Bank of England, on the different sums there specified; and which will be seen to be carried out in the column after the bare interest is subtracted from the gross charge in the middle column. the first column containing the principal, with the rate per cent. from the Commissioners' Public Accounts 1786. Appendix No. 1, page 70.

Principal

	Principal Debt.			Manag. & Interest			Manag. only.		
	£.	s.	d.	£.	s.	d.	£.	s.	d.
	1,836,275	17	10	136,453	12	8			
	67,155	8	2	8,195	12	0			
	2,200	0	0						
	18,000	0	0	0,540	0	0			
3 per Cent.	3,200,000	0	0	97,285	14	4			
				96,000	0	0	1,285	14	4
Ditto	1,000,000	0	0	30,401	15	8			
				30,000	0	0	401	15	8
Ditto	3,200,000	0	0	100,000	0	0			
				96,000	0	0			
Ditto	500,000	0	0	15,000	0	0	4,000	0	0
				50,000	0	0			
Ditto	4,000,000	0	0	121,898	3	5			
				120,000	0	0			
Ditto	1,250,000	0	0	37,500	0	0	1,898	3	5
				37,500	0	0			
Ditto	1,750,000	0	0	54,500	0	0			
				52,500	0	0			
Ditto	986,800	0	0	29,604	0	0			
				29,604	0	0			
Ditto	107,389,696	5	1	3,282,241	8	10			
				3,221,990	17	8½	60	5	11
Ditto	37,340,073	16	4	1,141,206	5	0½			
				1,120,202	4	5½			
4 per Cent.	32,750,000	0	0	1,328,421	17		21,003	15	9
				1,310	00	0			
5 per Cent.	6,879,341	19	6	347,834	14		18,421	17	6
				343,967	2	0			
Ditto	10,990,651	10	4	549,532	11	6	3,869	12	6
				549,502	11	6			
3 per Cent.	24,065,084	13	11½	735.97	13	0			
				721.902	1	0½			
Ditto	1,919,600	0	0	58,6	15		14,022	3	1¼
				57,588	0	0			
							1,079	15	6
Total	£.239,154,879	12	4						

Funded Debt 1786.

Page 28 Commissioners' Accounts, Charges on Aggregate Fund — — —   64,600 0 0

By omission in Management, page 69, carried to
   page 28, Commissioners' Accounts — 8,819 0 0

£.199,658 8 11

Amount of Management on a Debt accumulated by Mr. Pitt, funded and unfunded, which when converted into 3 per Cents. will be 211,000,000l. Management at 450l. per Million — — —   94,500 0 0
   10,000 0 0

New Aggregate Fund £.304,168 8 11

Charge of Management (Brought over)	£.304,168	8	11
Liberal allowance (say 30 Clerks at 500l. per Annum)	15,000	0	0
Amount of the extortionate Charge made by the Bank of England for Transfers and Payment of Dividends — — —	£.289,168	8	11

The arguments in favour of the Bank of England can be only in this kind of language, 'that there is a great deal of work, and that a great deal of money ought to be paid.' But to bring this business home to the nearest certainty, I refer the reader to the next page, where he will find the days of transfer, and that the whole time of attendance is in some of the departments but five hours in the week, and in others not more than two hours, by the time allowance is made for the forty holidays; a clear proof how trifling the real money transfers are, comparatively speaking, with that business done almost every day by the blood-sucking hounds in the Alley. But the fact is, when these villains see it their interest to extend their game, we are amused by our government with the idea of flourishing times, increase of money, increase of trade, &c. when in fact it is increase of paper credit, increase of swindling in the den of thieves—and poor John pays the piper!

Transfer Days, Payments of Dividends, and proper Hours for transacting each Day's Business.

Names.	Days of Transfer.	Hours.	Dividends when due.	Hours for rec. Div.
Bank Stock.	Tuesd. Thursd. Friday	11 to 1	Lady-Day and Mich.	9 to 11 and 1 to 3*
5 per Cent. Navy Anns.	Monday, Wed. Friday	Ditto	Midsum. and Christ.	Ditto
4 per Cent. Consolidated	Tues. Thurs. Fri. Sat.	Ditto	Lady. Day and Mich.	Ditto
3 per Cent. Consolidated	Tues. Wed. Thur. Fri.	Ditto	Midsum. and Christ.	9 to 3
Reduced	Ditto	Ditto	Lady-Day and Mich.	9 to 11 and 1 to 3
1726	Tuesday and Thursday	Ditto	Midsum. and Christ.	Ditto
Long Annuities	Tuesday, Wed. Sat .r.	Ditto	Lady-Day and Mich.	Ditto
Short Annuities 1777	Wednesday and Saturd.	Ditto	Ditto	Ditto
Short Annuities 1780	Mond. Wed. Friday	Ditto	Ditto	Ditto
South-Sea Stock	Ditto	12 to 1	Midsum. and Christ.	9 to 12
3 per Cent. Old Annuit.	Ditto	Ditto	Lady-Day and Mich.	Ditto
New Annuities	Tuesd. Thur. Saturday	Ditto	Midsum. and Christ.	Ditto
1751	Tuesday and Thursday	Ditto	Ditto	Ditto
India Stock	Tuesd. Thur. Saturday	Ditto	Ditto	9 to 2
Annuities	Mond. Wed. Friday	Ditto	Lady-Day and Mich.	Ditto

* Saturdays after One excepted.

There is not any bufinefs tranfacted at the Bank of England on the following days:—January 1, 6, 18, 25, 30. February 2, 24. March 25. April 25. May 1, 29. June 4, 11, 24, 29. July 25. Auguft 12, 24. Sept. 2, 21, 22, 29. October 18, 25, 28. November 1, 4, 5, 9, 30. December 21, 25, 26, 27, 28;---and if any of thefe days happen on a Sunday, they are kept on the Monday. Afh-Wednefday, Good-Friday, Eafter-Monday and Tuefday, and Whit Monday and Tuefday are alfo kept as holidays.

Having ftated the confequent effects of funding, prior to the year 1786, I come now to explain what hath been the conduct of our prefent heaven-born Minifter, as a financier for the country.

Abftract from the Commiffioners' Public Accounts, publifhed 21ft March 1786, page 72.

Bank of England, March 2, 1786.
Account of Navy, Victualling, and Tranfport Bills, and Ordnance Debentures, converted into 5 per Cent. Annuities at the Bank of England, agreeable to an Act of the laft Seffion of Parliament:

	Amount of Bills			5 per Cent. Stock		
	£.	s.	d.	£.	s.	d.
Navy	6,401,423	0	9	7,131,181	1	3
Victualling	2,925,804	4	4	3,259,343	1	4
Ordnance	0,538,714	13	3	0,600,127	7	9
	£.9,865,941	18	4	£.10,990,651	10	4

A. NEWLAND, Chief Cafhier.

Amount of Bills paid   9,865,941   18   4

Total Amount £.1,124,709 12 0

Which fum is, by the extortion of the corporation of money-locufts, faddled immediately as a mortgage on the labour of induftry, bearing an intereft of 5l. per cent. for ever.

State of the public debt prior to Mr. Pitt's funding, including the first 10,990,651l. 10s. 4d. funded by himself:

	Amount of Stock Debt 1786.		Amount of Stock Debt reduced to Sterling, at the price current of the day.		
	£.	£.	£.	s.	d.
3 per Cents.	188,534,877	at 55½	104,165,625	0	9
4 Ditto	32,750,000	at 75	24,562,500	0	3
5 Ditto	17,869,992	at 93¼	16,753,117	0	0
	£.239,154,869		£.145,481,242	0	9

This may be supposed to be the utmost amount of money received for the above funded securities — £.145,481,242 0 9

As I would wish the money-lenders to have justice done them, as well as the public, I would allow, to make good to such as may have purchased at higher premiums, and holders of real property, the sum of — 20,000,000 0 0

£.165,481,242 0 9

Hence it plainly appears, that after doing the strictest justice to all the parties, no more than the above sum of 165,481,242l. 0s. 9d. is due from the public, exclusive of 1,193l,674l. 7s. 3d. on annuities; and if the present stock be reduced to sterling, and an interest paid of 4l. per cent. the whole amount of annual interest wou'd have been no more than 6,619,249l. 14s. 0d.¼

Subtracting this sum from our present expenditure in interest, which is £.8,073,265 19 11
6,619,249 14 0

If this reformation had then taken place, the annual saving would have amounted to £.1,454,016 5 11

In

In the Guardian of Public Credit, publifhed in 1788, there is a table of figures that proves that the above fum will produce in the 4l. per cents. with compound intereft, in 43 years £.168,145,678 13 11
Sterling amount of the Debt,
as it then ftood   -   165,481,242 10 9

£. 2,664,436 3 2

From this reafonable compromife, the whole debt would have been difcharged in 43 years with a peace eftablifhment, without an additional fhilling in new taxes. But the cafe is now altered; as Mr. Pitt's funding and debts unfunded, if the whole were converted into the 3l. per cent. would amount to at leaft £.211,000,000! which caufes an additional expence in the management (at the ufual rate of 450l. per million) of 94,950l. and no addition for aggregate.

But notwithftanding all this, the author is furnifhed with fuch new information refpecting the extravagant abufe in the public income and expenditure, that a fuitable reformation taking place, the people may be reftored to their natural rights refpecting the price of provifions, and ftill a more rapid progrefs may be made in liquidating the debt.

In thefe two departments alone no man can deny my affertion, when I faid the debt had been once paid prior to Mr. Pitt's funding, with a reafonable intereft of 4l. per cent. per annum. I allude to the annuities, for which no money was received.

£.1,193,674 7 3

A fum annually extorted by the Bank of England for management. I fay extorted, becaufe 10,000l. would have been an ample reward   —   189,668 8 1

£.1,383,242 15 2

Hence

Hence it appears, that the above annual payments were made out of the public purse, for which no money had been received; for proof of this, look at the Commissioners' Accounts page 70, published in 1786. This is a fact that cannot be denied even by such as insist on the justice and necessity of wars; so that it is a clear case that the enormous debt was needless, and established by the means of crafty swindling.

No plan can be framed to support the extravagancies of Mr. Pitt in the publick expenditure, as he hath so enormously exceeded all others. I shall in a future page state the increase of the burthens occasioned by the monopoly of the Bank of England, which may be avoided in future by establishing a Bank or Banks for the benefit of the publick, instead of leaving them in the jaws of these devouring locusts. Some people (whose ideas are very short of the fact) have asserted, that Government Banking would be the greatest of all monopolies; but that I deny—for in the case of the government of a country banking to support the public expenditure, every man is a banker, and shares in the profits; therefore it cannot be a monopoly. The present Bank of England obtains considerably more than three millions annually for the loan of paper!

As the clearest proof of the practicability of banking for the benefit of the public, I refer to a statement of an establishment of this kind in one of the provinces of America; taken from the Sunday Monitor, 31st Jan. 1796:

"The Assembly in Pennsylvania was opened the 4th of December, by a very luminous speech from their Governor, Mifflen, wherein he describes their situation as flourishing beyond the example of any country on record. So far from being under the necessity of imposing taxes on the people, or borrowing money, he states, that in a very short period the money in their Bank will amount to such a sum, that the interest alone will

will not only pay all the expences of Government, but go a great way in making their public roads, bridges, and canals."

This, I have reason to believe, took its foundation in consequence of my publishing the Guardian of Public Credit in the year 1788: for when I heard they were upon a proposition of funding money, I sent a copy of my work to an eminent character, forewarning them of the evil tendency of funding money.

And as a further information to my own countrymen, I see it necessary to bring forward a statement I have made, by converting the Stock Debt into sterling; by which I shall prove another increase of the public debt, for which no money was received.

Brought forward amount of Stock Debt, 1786, as stated in a former page.

Stock Debt converted into Sterling, agreeable to the price of the day.

	L.	L.	S. D.
3 per cents.	188,554,887 at 55¼	104,165,615	0 9
4 do.	32,750,000 at 75	24,562,500	0 0
5 do.	17,869,992 at 93¾	16,753,117	0 0

239,154,879
Total amount of Sterling, 1786 145,481,242 0 9

The following statement will prove the increase of the debt from the year 1786 to 1794, and for which no money was received.

Amount of Stock   at the present price converted into Sterling

	L.	now worth	L.	S. D.
3 per cents.	188,554,887	94	177,222,783	15 4
4 do.	32,750,000	103¼	33,814,375	0 0
5 do.	17,869,992	120	21,443,990	8 0
Original Amount of Stock Debt	239,154,879			

Amount

Amount of Stock Debt converted
into Sterling, 1794, ——   232,481, 49   3 4
Amount of Stock Debt converted
into Sterling, as it stood 1786;
and which may be estimated to the
full value of the money received   145,481,242   0 9
                                   ─────────────────
                                    86,999,907   2 7

Amount of debt increased on the public on account of stock-jobbing, and for which no money was received, say eighty-six millions, nine hundred ninety-nine thousand, nine hundred and seven pounds, two shillings and seven pence.

But we are told by the crafty stock-jobber, that it is the increase of national credit. Will he prove an additional guinea being brought into the kingdom? No: but a considerable decrease is the fact; as the Dutch and other foreigners in the interim took the advantage, and sold out of our funds to the amount of 900,000l. and on which they procured a profit of 400,000l. at least, that never can return to this country. And all this might have been avoided, provided the advantage of paper circulation had been secured for the benefit of the Public instead of the Directors of the Bank of England and other monopolizers. Note, a principal reason why the increase in the debt to this enormous amount took place, was because from the year 1786 to the year 1792 little or no money was borrowed; which must appear strangely paradoxical to such as have not the ability or the will to investigate: but from the above circumstance the loan mongers had money to receive, and as soon as the change took place in consequence of the war, the Minister wanting money, they had to advance twenty times the sum, and stocks tumbled down nearly to the price they were at on the conclusion of the American War.——I think I may venture to say that the present war is nearly at
                                                             an

an end, as the money has been all exhausted for some time; and that paper credit is rapidly coming into that contempt it deserves. The sooner the better; as from its present operations in the increase of plundering the most distressed part of the community. I would advise the few that may have cash to spare, to be cautious how they deal in the rotten fabric of the funds, that they may avoid purchasing stock at advanced prices: for, depend upon it, the eyes of the people will soon be open; if not, the peace will by no means ease the public burthens; for what has been the fact will soon follow, an extravagant increase of the debt at the rate perhaps of 40 or 50 per cent. increasing a capital of at least one hundred and fifty millions, for which no money has been received: therefore the patience of the people will not continue to bear it. And let me further inform you, that what hath been advanced, hath been seven-eighths at least in new coinage of paper

Now, my Fellow Citizens, let me intreat you who have abilities, to investigate, and you will be able to convey such facts to the plundered public, as no doubt will rouse them from their present lethargy.

It was remarked, that soon after Mr. Pitt got into administration he made twenty thousand pounds by a single lift in the funds: and no doubt but he has continued his stock-jobbing pursuits with equal success. Lord Charles Catchpenny, now Earl of L———, King Harry of Scotland; all this in addition to their lucrative places and pensions. It has been remarked, that Boyd and Benfield, the noted loan-mongers, a few years since were men of very narrow capitals, now in possession of immense tracts of the finest lands in the kingdom, and hold their whole neighbourhood in subordination to them; and all this acquired by loan mongering and stock jobbing. I could single out many more objects of this kind, wallowing in the public plunder; but shall content myself at present
with

with saying, there are but few of the bankers and fat aldermen that have not greased their sides with this kind of plunder. Playthings are created, unnecessary horses and dogs innumerable, and on which no restraint is laid on their feeding.

The new project of payment of the funded debt never entered the heart of any man in this kingdom, nor perhaps the universe, till it entered into the head of our immaculate minister. I have therefore now to proceed to prove Mr. Pitt, as I have before stated, borrowed of the Bank of England, in the year 1786, 9,865,941l. 18s. 4d. and for which he gave securities in the 5l. per cent. for 10,990,65 l. 10s. 4d. as under you have the particulars of his proceedings in the purchase of stock. Copied from the Sun, 13th February, 1794.

An Account of the present State of the Money laid out to reduce the National Debt.

	Sums bought in.	Sums paid.		
	L.	L.	S.	D.
Consols, 3 per cent.	4,943,755	3,819,395	19	6
Reduced —	3,575,100	2,848,585	19	3
Old South Sea	1,939,650	1,540,6:0	8	9
New South Sea	1,506,000	1,207,017	11	9
South Sea —	452,000	362,596	7	6
Amount of the Funded Debt bought in	12,416,505			
Total amount of sums paid		9,778,246	6	9

The foregoing statement seems intended to prove to the public the wonderful operation the minister hath made in lessening the funded debt by discharging in the 3 per cents. — 12,416,505
with the sum only of sterling money to the amount of —— 9,778,246 6 9

2,638,258 13 3

There, fay the advocates for the immaculate minifter, there is a financier for you; notice that he hath faved for the public 2,638,258l. 13s. 3d. Confiftent with Mr. Pitt's invariable practice, here is another bit of backftairs work—another fample of his deception: he borrowed in the 5 per cents. and paid in the 3 per cents. In order to fet the public right refpecting this important deception, it is neceffary to put this plain queftion in common arithmetic—If 10,990,651l. 10s. 4d. fecured an annual intereft of 549,532l. 11s. 6d. what fecurities muft have been given in the 3 per cents. to have obtained the fame annual intereft?— The anfwer is   — —   18,317,752 10 7

Now I come to the real fact, as to progrefs in leffening the debt

      9,778,246   6   9
Cafh to buy   87,695   11   7

Remains   9,865,941   18   4
fterling, with which 12,416,505l. is bought up in the 3 per cents. But there ftill remains in the hands of the Minifter a balance of 87,695l. 11s. 7d. Now I fhall give him credit at the rate of 78l. 15s. per cent. which is the rate he has been paying 111,334l. 18s. 11d. making a total of   ——   12,527,839 18 11

      Total lofs   5,789,912 11   8
in the 3 per cents. of the minifter's new project of buying and felling money.

Note, that 1,865,941l. 18s. 4d. was borrowed and expended in the payment of 12,527,839l. 8s. 11d. and by this buying and felling of money Mr. Pitt created an additional debt in the 3 per cents. to the amount of 5,789,912l. 11s. 8d. from the circumftance alone of his buying and felling money; and that by the
                time

time every expence is added to this fingular tranfaction, the public lofs will be more than fix millions fterling: and provided he, Mr. Pitt, is fuffered
to go on in his mad career of buying and felling money, more than fixty millions will be loft to the public
on account of money borrowed by himfelf.

	L.	s.
The average paid by Mr. Pitt in the 3 per cents. was	78	15
The proportion of his 5 per cents. when converted into 3 per cents. was no more than	54	0
	24	15

Coft of Premiums for the borrowing and
paying   54l.   is   24 15 0   what is the coft of
do. on 27   is   12   7 6   100l. fterling
do. on 13   is   6   3 9
do. on   4l. 10s. is 2   1 3
do. on   1   0 is   9 2

Sterling 100 0   45 16 8 Amount of premiums paid by Mr. Pitt on every hundred pounds
fterling, exclufive of 5l. 11s. intereft; as it appears
that the foregoing fum of 9,865,941l. 18s. 4d. coft
more by 1l. 10s. than if it had refted in Navy, Victualling, and Tranfport Bills, it is but fair to charge
the additional expence accumulated by additional intereft. Note, that 1l. 10s. per annum on 9,865,941l.
18s. 4d. is 147,684l. 8s. 4d. But as this annual
charge has a gradual decline as the payment takes
place, in order to avoid loading the reader as much
as poffible with too many figures, I will average the
additional lofs for the two firft years, which will amount
at leaft to 270,000l. and the fum the minifter paid
took at leaft eight years in the profecution. It is
fpeaking within compafs to fay that 900,000l. fterling
was the additional expence incurred by additional
intereft; and that this fum, when converted into the

3 per

3 per cents. will, allowing the proportion the minister received, amount to as under.

	L. s.		L.	S.	D.
	54 0		900,000	0	0
	27 0		450,000	0	0
	13 10		225,000	0	0
	4 10		75,000	0	0
	1 0		16,666	13	4
	100 0				

Amount of the above sum of 900,000l. when converted into 3 per cents.   1,666,666 13 4

Amount of the loss in premiums in the proportion to what Mr. Pitt had been paying, that is to say, 45l. 16s. 8d. per cent. ———   5,789,912 11 8

Additional debt incurred by premiums ——— ———   7,456,579 5 0

As under, the above stock is converted into sterling, in order to give the reader a more accurate view of the sum wasted to carry on the deception, at the same proportion the minister had been paying 78l. 15s. per cent.

L. s.	L. s.		L.	s.	D.
50 per cent. on	7,456,579 5	is	3,728,289	12	6
25 do. on	do.	is	1,864,144	16	3
3 15 do. on	do.	is	93,206	4	10
Total amount at 78l. 15s. per cent.			5,685,640	13	7

This, with commission, brokerage, &c. cannot be less than six millions sterling total loss, in order to carry on the deception of lessening the funded debt: But it does not end here, as some considerable loss must have taken place since the 13th February, 1794.

I am

I am not informed as to particulars, but recollect that Mr. Pitt, winding up his financial career in the laſt Parliament, ſaid that he congratulated the country on the circumſtance of his having 2,400,000l. for the continuance of liquidating the debt. If this was really the caſe, why not borrow 2,400,000l. the leſs? as the expence then in borrowing and paying was 14l. 11s. per cent. the average of the expence, including the loan for the Emperor. *Quære*, What is the amount of 14l. 11s. per cent. on 22,800,000l? — *Anſwer* 3,317,400l. Now the fact is, that if he had ſtated the circumſtance in plain Engliſh, he might have given a glance on his brother loan-mongers, and told them by this conduct that he had ſwindled the country out of another ſum to the amount of 343,700l. which was identically the fact.

When I publiſhed the Guardian of Public Credit in 1788, I alluded to the uſurious contract ſigned March 2d. 1786, in which ſecurities were given in the 5l. per cents. for   £.10,990,651 10 4
To pay Navy and Victualling
    Bills, and Ordnance Deben-
    tures, to the amount of   £. 9,865,941 18 4

Bank of England's profit by this
    one Contract with the Public   £.1,124,709, 12 0
In addition to this nearly 200,000l. per annum charged for the management of the debt, which could not coſt them a twentieth part of that ſum, as it is only for payment of dividends and transfers, (for which latter refer to the table that ſtates days of transfer, page 7 in this work, and you will find that not more than five hours in the week is occupied by that part of the buſineſs) I proved the inconveniency of money being monopolized by the Bank of England, and that it had the ſame effect on the people reſpecting uſury and extortion, as the price of grain would be affected, provided the whole crop grown in one pariſh were in

the hands of one farmer. The Bank of England, fearing that this kind of information would come into general knowledge, stopped their former mode of proceeding, and have not appeared openly in any one contract for a loan since my former work; but have increased that part of their business that may be called pawn-broking, for which I believe this honourable Company have never taken out a licence, therefore I should suppose them liable to pay the several penalties.

This pawn-broking business I find is carried on in the following manner:—As the loans are always made good by instalments, when a single payment is made of 10l. or 15l. per cent. the memorandum acknowledging the payment is called Scrip, and is by the Bank of England deemed a security for the sums that have been paid. The loan-monger takes this scrip to the Bank of England, and in part or in all makes an exchange for their paper, and for which the Bank of England charge an interest of 5l. per cent. This enables the pawners of scrip to make their second payments, which intitles them to a second scrip; and so they may go on making their deposits, and constantly pawning up home to the payment of their last dividend that completes the contract.

There being no more at the present period than fifteen millions of specie in the kingdom, I cannot give credit to the Bank of England and private bankers for more than 6,000,000l. When 22,800,000l. is funded, is there a possibility of completing this contract, without the help of 16,800,000l. Bank of England paper? Who then are we to suppose to be the masters and commanders of the interest and premiums for the loan of a little money and a great deal of paper, but these Directors of the Bank of England; as not a single loan can be completed without the aid of their paper, at least three fourths? And can we suppose that they do not take the advantage of so much

much of the profitable loans as they find convenient for themselves, though they never openly appeared in any one contract since the year 1786; though more than sixty millions have been contracted for in about the space of one year, by an individual who but a few years since did not possess property to the amount of a ten thousandth part of the sums contracted for?

From the circumstance of such immense sums contracted for by Boyd and Benfield, the craft of the Bank of England may be easily perceived; that it is in order to hide from the public eye their being so deeply concerned in the iniquitous practice of usury and extortion, which must be added to the advantages they make of their immense circulating paper; which, by a moderate computation, cannot be less than from sixty to seventy millions, producing them an annual profit of between three and four millions.

Terms of the Loan of 22,800,000l. of which the Emperor was to have a part.

The subscribers were to have

		L.	s.	D.
3l. per cents. at 75 producing an annual interest of	- -	2	5	0
4l. per cents. at 25	- -	1	0	0
0 6 4½ Long Anns.		0	6	4½
20 16 8 Imperial Loan		0	12	6
2l. 1s. 5d. per annum, for 25 years, equal to a perpetuity of	-	0	17	6
		5	1	4½

5l. 1s. 4d. annual interest bears a proportion of 59l. in the 3 per cents. of course (the 3 per cents. being at 63l.) the price of the day produced a profit of - -   L. s. D.   4 0 0

Commission allowed to the subscribers 2l. per cent. interest bearing date before the payments were completed
2l. 0 0 - -   4 0 0

                       8 0 0

The 3 per cents. were then at 63l.
Prófit to the fubfcribers   8
_____

Amount paid into the Exchequer 55l.

If 55l. produce a profit of 8l. what will 100l. produce?

L.	S.	L.	S.
55	0	8	0
27	10	4	0
13	15	2	0
3	15	0	11

100   0   14   11 profit on one hundred pounds fterling, if the ftock had been fold the day it was contracted for at the then price current.

If 100l. produce a profit of 14l. 11s. what will 22,800,000l. produce? ' The anfwer is 3,317,400l. profit of one day to the loan-mongers.——It has been pofitively afferted that there were feveral individuals who made each of them a profit of 100,000l. by this fingle loan! Is not the paradoxical parable in the fcripture verified, that even the poor man who hath nothing fhall have it taken from him? Every one of thefe loans being an additional mortgage on the profits of his labour, of courfe made a facrifice before he has obtained it.

It appears that the above loan was not carried into effect, and that the following advantages were placed in favour of the Englifh loan; from which it may be eafily conceived that it was never intended to be repaid by the Emperor.

The fubfcribers were to have 83l. 6s. 8d. in the 3 per cents. and 5l. per cent. per annum for 25 years.

Payment

Payment to be made as follows:

1st November 1794	10l. per cent.
17th April 1795	10l. ditto
10th June	10l. ditto
17th July	10l. ditto
28th August	15l. ditto
23d October	15l. ditto
27th November	15l. ditto
15th January 1796	15l. ditto
	100l.

The interest of this loan was said at one time to take place the preceding May, but there have been so many shiftings and changings taking place, that it is difficult to say when; but in all doubtful cases I shall lean in favour of the contract. As I do not mean to exaggerate the amount as to the causes of complaint, I shall only charge the commencement of the interest from the 1st of November 1794, which is the time the first payments take place; and as the time from the 1st of November 1794 to the 15th of January 1796 is fourteen months and 15 days, the interest to the subscribers from the proportion of cash in their hands, advantages will accrue to the amount of 6l. per cent. they being in the receipts of 7l. 10s. per cent. per annum, as the above different periods commence before their payments are completed.

Proof that the annual interest bears 7l. 10s.

83l. 6s. 8d. in the 3 per cents. is	2 10 0
Annuities for 25 years, at	5 0 0
	£.7 10 0

Amount of the annual charge for this extraordinary loan.

Brought

Brought over proof of profits obtained by this loan, by the interest taking place before the payments were completed   L. s. D.
                                                                              6   0   0
       Usual commission 2l. per cent.
       Discount   2l.   4   0   0
                                                               10   0   0

Hence it appears, that before the payments were completed there was a profit to the subscriber of 10l. per cent. of course no more can be received into the Exchequer than 90l. per cent. Quere, what then is the annual charge on the above 90l?

       Stock in the 3 per cents. 83l. 6s. 8d.   L. s. D.
         annual interest   -   -   2 10 0
       5l. on 90l. per cent. being equal to a
         perpetuity of 4l. per annum   4   0   0
                                                          6 10 0

Quere, If 6l. 10s. per annum be worth 90l. what is 3l. per annum worth?—Answer 41l. 10s. 8d.

To estimate the expence of the payment of this loan: Agreeable to Mr. Pitt's practice of lessening the funded debt, the 4,800,000l. lent the Emperor will cost nearly double, exclusive of the extravagant interest; and as we may suppose it to be received as the price of blood, who then is to pay it, the Emperor, or poor broken-backed John Bull?—Now suppose Mr. Pitt had been a subscriber to this curious loan, with the 2,400,000l. he boasted to have in his hands, instead of buying up in our 3 per cents. at 63l. what would have been the difference to this country?

                                                        L.   S.   D.
                                                        63   0   0
                                                        41 10   8

Profit obtained by the Emperor's Loan   21   9   4

                                                                          Profit

Profit by purchasing in the Emperor's Loan.

	L.	S.	D.		L.	S.	D.
On	41	10	8		21	9	4
	41	10	8		21	9	4
	10	7	8		5	7	4
	5	3	10		2	13	10
	1	7	2		0	13	2
	100	0	0		51	13	0

It now clearly appears that if Mr. Pitt had been a contributor to the Emperor's loan, instead of buying up in our 3 per cents. at 63l. the saving would have been 51l. 13s. on every hundred pounds. The next thing I have to prove is the total amount of savings on the 2,400,000l.

L. S.			L.		L.
51 13 per cent.	on	1,000,000	is	516,500
Ditto		on	1,000,000	is	516,500
Ditto		on	400,000	is	206,600
			2,400,000		1,239,600

From this statement it clearly appears that there was a double choice for Mr. Pitt to have made; in the first instance he might have saved 343,700l. by funding a less sum in our 3 per cents. or if he had been a contributor to the Emperor's loan to the amount of the above 2,400,000l. he might have saved 1,239,600l. This would have been the saving in either case, whether the money be repaid by the Emperor or this country.

Contracts composed of such complex sums, whose value perpetually fluctuates, through the arts of the avaricious gambler or stock-jobber, the ignorance or indifference of interested Ministerial agents, or the perplexed and improvident conduct of the financial administration, must naturally lie out of the immediate address of persons who do not bestow much labour and time on the study of a very dry
subject;

subject; but it requires no further argument to prove that if dealings were meant to be conducted fairly, and for the public advantage, they would naturally be divested of this perplexing complexity, which can answer no other end than to veil the wasteful transactions from the public eye.

Effects of the Emperor's Loan, continued:—

Though I consider precision an ornament to every public performance, I wish to curtail as much as possible that dull part of my work figures; though I have now an estimate by me that proves what I have to say respecting this extravagant and unparalleled loan. It is a fact commonly understood, that one hundred pounds, or any sum of money, in the situation of compound interest, will double itself in fourteen or fifteen years. The following short explanation I imagine will satisfy my readers respecting the further effects of the loan in this country nick-named the Emperor's loan:—I have proved clearly that no more than 9ol. for 100l. can be received into the Exchequer, allowing 7l. 10s. annually for the first twenty-five years on the sum of 4,800,000l. taking it at the rate of 4 per cent. interest, the principal and interest is paid the first fifteen years and a half.

Note, that the surplus of 4 per cent. on compound interest is sufficient to discharge the principal; quere, at the end of fifteen years and a half, how stands the case with the public? they are still indebted 83l. os. 8d. per cent. in the 3 per cents. on the whole amount of the sum borrowed 4,800,000l.

Quere, What is the proportion of 83l. 6s. 8d. per cent. on 4,800,000l? the answer is 4,000,000l. bearing an annual interest of 3 per cent with the additional annual interest of 5 per cent. for 9 years and a half; so that the commissioners may say, in liquidating the debt in the year 1812, as they did in the year 178 , that no money was received for the following annual charge; that is,

On

                                        L.
On 4,800,000l. at 5 per cent. is   280,000
On 4,000,000l. at 3 per cent. is   120,000
                                  ─────────
                                   400,000

This is an annual charge from the firſt fifteen years and half to the twenty-fifth year, leaving then a further incumbrance of 400,000l. in the 3 per cents. to be diſcharged, or an annual intereſt to be continued for ever on it, until ſuch time as the principal is paid.

Leſt I ſhould have been too ſhort in my explanation, I now repeat that the above ſum of 400,000l. annually will be paid for nine years and a half, and a further ſum of 4,000,000l. in the 3 per cents. for which no money was ever received either by the Emperor or the people of this country.

Will not poſterity ſtartle, and ſay, ' What, nothing done for all this money!' I think there was enough done;—between two and three hundred thouſand French and Auſtrians were murdered in Germany, for the ſupport of the Chriſtian religion! If England ſhould at that period be governed by monks and friars, no doubt but Billy Pitt will be canonized for the part he took in the holy cruſade.

Now let me aſk my countrymen whether there is an inſtance of any young profligate having through the exceſs of gaming, drinking, whoring, and all the vices that could be collected together, ever made more rapid ſtrides in the deſtruction of his own paternal eſtate, than Mr. Pitt hath had the impudence to do with the public eſtate of this country.

Now for Mr. Pitt's general funding. First was the peace establishment in 1786, at 5 per cent.

	L.	s.	D.
The peace establishment in 1786, at 5 per cent.	10,990,651	10	4
To carry on the iniquitous war 1793, sterling amount	4,500,000	0	0
1794, Ditto	11,000,000	0	0
1795, Ditto	18,000,000	0	0
Ditto for the Emperor	4,800,000	0	0
Ditto English	18,000,000	0	0
1796, Ditto for the Navy	3,536,422	0	0
Ditto 16th of April	7,500,000	0	0
	78,327,073	10	4

Mr. Morgan at this period by calculations converted the whole of the funded debt into the 3 per cents. which he said produced a capital of 410,944,685l. and for which I can see no other reason than that of making the calculation more easy for the reader. It is strange that Mr. Morgan or any other person in the character of a sensible gentleman, should talk of saving by converting one stock into another; as every man that will investigate this important business must see that no reduction can take place in the funded debt, unless you bridle the stock-jobbers by a consolidated compromise with the funded creditor.— Referring again to Mr. Pitt's expenditure, he is now in want of 40,000,000 0 0

According to the general practice of funding, there will be then unprovided for at the least 10,000,000 0 0

£.128,327,073 10 4

Brought over, expended by Mr. Pitt,
sterling amount — 128,327,073 10 4

Mr. Pitt's expenditure converted into the 3 per cent.
Average at the most he received.

	L.	s.	D.
56 per cent.	128,327,073	10	4
28 do.	64,163,536	15	2
14 do.	32,081,768	7	7
2 do	4,587,109	15	$4\frac{1}{2}$

Total amount 100 in 3 per cent. 229,159,488 8 $5\frac{1}{2}$
Vansittart's estimate of Mr. Pitt's
having paid in ditto — 18,001,685 0 $0\frac{1}{2}$

Created, and to be created, by
the time all the money is funded
that hath been expended by Mr.
Pitt — — 211,157,833 8 5

Amount of annual interest on the new   L.   S. D.
debt created by Mr Pitt at 3 per cent. 6,334,735 0 1
Additional charge of management by
the Bank of England, at the rate of
450l. per million, on the new capital
created — — 94,500 0 0

6,429,235 0 1

This is the progress of our immaculate minister, in order to ease the burthens of the people: he hath brought an increase of expenditure on interest alone to the above amount of 6,429,235l. 0s. 1d.

The enormity of this wickedness could not have arrived to such a pitch if he had not persuaded our lazy landholders that they had no right to call gentlemen to account that were high in office. Thus they
were

were from their conduct fuppofed to believe: but I think the very reverfe; and that a Minifter of State is as liable to be called to account for the embezzlement of public money as any other officer under the Crown; and I am ready to bring forward the impeachment. But at prefent fhall leave the enormous capital of 211,157,853l. 8s. 5d. and refer to that part of the fwindling bufinefs of buying and felling money, by which the Public were tricked out of fix millions fterling; and in another fingle and more recent inftance to the amount of 343,700l. This laft, in point of conviction, is exactly fimilar to the proof brought againft the fheriff's-officer for the ftealing of two ducks from a perfon that he had arrefted at Belfont. The officer boafted of this wickednefs as he was coming to town in a coach with another perfon, and this was the means of bringing him to trial and conviction; and he was fentenced to tranfportation for feven years. Similar to this, Mr. Pitt boafted of his wickednefs openly in the Houfe of Commons, declaring pofitively that he had 2,400,000l. to leffen the funded debt. As fure as the perfon at Belfont loft his ducks, fo fure the public were fwindled out of the 343,700l. by the tranfaction of Mr. Pitt funding 2,400,000l. more than was wanted. That this boafted declaration took place can be proved, I fuppofe, at leaft by one hundred honourable gentlemen then in the Houfe of Commons.

The officer, I have obferved before, was fentenced to tranfportation for feven years for ftealing the two ducks, and poor Ifaac Moore was hanged in the year 1793 for ftealing a 10l. bank-note out of a letter: What then muft be done with our heaven-born minifter for taking the active part in that tranfaction that fwindled the public out of 343,700l.? If the minifter has his reward on conviction, all other impeachments againft him will be needlefs, and confiderable expences faved.

Two

Two writers have lately taken up the difcuffion of the financial operations of the prefent minifter on oppofite grounds—Mr. Morgan, who reprobates, and Mr. Vanfittart, who defends, the minifter's meafures. Since thefe pamphlets have come abroad, the public mind feems to have been much divided upon the merits of their refpective affertions and arguments. But the extraordinary circumftances of the Bank of England, and the late failures; others fo much to be apprehended; the confultations of the minifter with feveral opulent, commonly called monied, men, more properly circulators of paper medium; and the meafures faid to be in agitation for an extravagant increafe of this kind of fpecie; has proved too clearly the full truth of Mr. Morgan's calculations, although he has not reached to the extremity of thofe evils and abufes which he profeffed to expofe in his prefent tract.— I mean to touch upon fome of the leading points of thofe gentlemen, and to fhew how far fhort of the reality Mr. Morgan has eftimated the extravagance and wafte of the minifter; and to expofe the delufive, artful, and unfair reafoning and calculations of Mr. Vanfittart. The loans of the prefent compared with the moft extravagant of paft wars, the ftate and management of the national debt and finking fund, and their effects on the country, are the topics of Mr. Morgan's ferious lamentation and juft apprehenfions: Mr. Vanfittart attempts to argue away his conclufions, and contemn his w ll-grounded fears. It is meant here to examine the leading facts of both writers, and offer fuch reafoning as muft prove that though Mr. Morgan has calculated too much in favour of the minifter's meafures, he is correct in ftating them to be the moft ruinous of any that this country or all hiftory can produce. His proof of new debt being funded, confiderably more than one hundred million, in fo fhort a period, is a proof of his affertion, that the extravagant expence has been the

moft

moſt ruinous that this country ever experienced; tho' he has not once mentioned the new, blindfolded, ſwindling bonus of the capital bearing intereſt before the money is paid; and this upon inveſtigation appears to be from 3 to 4 per cent. on the capital on the Emperor's loan: I have proved it to be 6 per cent.

I have in a former page remarked that ſhort-ſighted idea of Mr. Morgan, where he is planning to reduce the debt by converting one deſcription of ſtock into another. Let any man reaſon fairly on the ſubject, and I will aſk him where the difference can be, whether the debt be in the 3, 4, or 5 per cents. provided each ſtock bear a proportionable intereſt; and to effect this will be always in the power of the ſtock-jobber, ſtock-holder, &c. as long as the debt ſhall be ſuffered to fluctuate, and of courſe remain a game. The recent fact muſt be an undoubted proof of Mr. Pitt's having waſted ſix millions in the operation of diſcharging twelve millions in the 3 per cents. And what difficulty will there be in keeping the preſent enormous debt at bay, provided no reformation takes place in this department? For, as the twelve millions took eight years in the payment, how eaſy will it be in the courſe of every eight years to ſtrike out an artificial pretence for war, either with the French, Spaniards, Dutch, or Americans, and ſpend more money in ſix months preparations than was ſaved in the preceding eight or ten years peace? So that not only the preſent age, but poſterity muſt for ever remain in the ſame or a worſe ſituation, except a compromiſe between debtor and creditor, and a ſolid reformation in the management of the public income and expenditure.

But there is an additional confirmation of Mr. Pitt's profligacy. He contracts a loan in the 5 per cents. ſubjecting the inhabitants of this country to a fluctuating loſs of 40 or 50 per cent. at the very time

the

the Irish agent contracted a loan with this country in the 5 per cents. reserving the liberty of paying at par; is not this a proof, in addition to Mr. Morgan's charge of error, misconduct, wickedness, and incapacity?

Mr. Vanfittart seems to place himself in a kind of security that few or none will investigate, otherwise he would not have gone such lengths in false and unfair reasoning, with delusive arguments. In his 31ft page he says the public are indebted to Mr. Pitt for his savings, by a mutilation of Dr. Price's plan to a perpetual annuity of 585,812l. worth at 4 per cent. a capital of 14,646,312l. The reverse of this statement is the truth; and the plain fact is, that had the debt been suffered to remain in its original state, instead of the above stated sum, the savings would have been six millions, equal to a saving in perpetual annuities of 300,000l. annually, for the proof of which I refer back to page 11. Admitting that savings had taken place, how ridiculous it is to say that the public are indebted to Mr. Pitt; as they could only have been indebted to their own industry in raising the same.

In Mr. Vanfittart's third table, a statement is given of several loans during the present war, in order to display the moderate rate of interest at which the Minister hath made his contracts; but the table exhibits a palpable evidence of the want of sincerity, of regard for truth, and the spirit of delusion which characterizes the whole of the pamphlet. In page 17, the average of the loans of the present wars are at 4l. 10s. 9d.$\frac{1}{2}$ annual interest; in the preceding page sufficient evidence has been given of that misstatement, even independent of the Emperor's loan. In that table the following account appears:

	Borrowed.	Capital created including Anns. Consolidated.	Interest.		
	L.	L.	L.	S.	D.
1795	18,000,000	25,828,876	4	14	10
1796	18,000,000	27,351,336	4	14	0

Navy debt funded 1794   £.3,398,098
For which a capital was created in the 5 per cents. of   3,536,422
                              ─────────
                              £.138,324 bonus

over and above 5 per cent. an advantage of 1l. 15s. on account of interest bearing date before the payments were completed. A new-fangled deception of Mr. Pitt's Mr. Vansittart hath thought fit to leave out; indeed, it would not answer his purpose to have added to the interest from 3l. at 4 per cent. on account of the capital bearing date so many months before the payments were completed, commission and discount making altogether in interest considerably more than ten shillings per cent. which swells the interest at least to 5l. 5s. on a capital advanced of at least four-fifths paper.

The circumstance of the account delivered by A. Newland, the 2d of March 1786, to pay navy and victualling bills, and ordnance debentures, for which securities were given in the 5 per cents. to the amount of   -   £.10,990,651 10 4
  Amount of bills paid   9,865,941 18 4
                              ───────────────
Bonus for this day's contract £.1,124,709 12 0

Capital borrowed bearing an interest of 5l. 11s. for ever. The Emperor's loan (page 28 of this pamphlet) carried a capital into the Exchequer, at 41l. 10s. 8d. in the 3 per cents.—Bonus for the day on every 100l. subscribed, sterling money 51l. 10s. or an annual interest of 6l. 10s. per cent. These are circumstances that correspond so little with Mr. Vansittart's statement, that he has thought fit to leave them entirely out of the question; but they certainly prove want of sincerity and regard for truth, and a spirit of delusion.

Now for the glorious advantages that have been acquired by this country on account of this immense increase of public plunder. Notwithstanding the
                                                       failure

failure or fruſtration of every ſcheme of ambition and conqueſt which the Miniſter hath undertaken in the courſe of the preſent war, ſtill it is aſſerted, that at no period was the glory or proſperity of this country (under all the exiſting circumſtances) at a greater heighth; and Mr. Morgan, who hath charged them with error, miſconduct, wickedneſs, and incapacity, is affectedly cenſured for not entering into minute proofs of theſe plain facts; as though his declared object was to expoſe thoſe which related to financial operations only.

What then are the bleſſings which this country has derived from the preſent Miniſter, and where are the proofs of his capacity, his patriotiſm, or his virtues? Melancholy and deplorable will be the proſpect of that vaſt volume of miſeries which he has created. The mind is perplexed to fix upon a period leſs fatal or deſtructive than another in the whole career of the preſent war. Of the prior part of his ſtrange and extravagant courſe, there is the ſame difficulty to diſcover one act of public policy or legiſlative conduct, which can claim a title to candour, manlineſs, openneſs, or dignity; the early part of his adminiſtration would ſeem to be a kind of experimental courſe in all the arts of tergiverſation, political chicanery, and public deluſion, preparatory to the grand ſcene of wantonneſs and profligacy exhibited within the laſt four accurſed years.

Is the project of the conqueſt of France a proof of capacity? Have the conduct exhibited at Toulon and at Dunkirk, and the fate of the gallant Sombrueil and his companions at Quiberon, nothing of error, wickedneſs, miſconduct, or incapacity in them? Is not that Stadtholder who made ſo many ſacrifices to this country, againſt the voice of his own, during the American war—is his independence no proof of the miniſter's error, miſconduct, wickedneſs, and incapacity? Is not the triple alliance, and the partition of Poland, the subsidies to Prussia, and the subsequent counter-alliance of that country with France, proofs of the Minister's error, misconduct, wickedness, and incapacity? Have we not at sea 110 ships of the line, 18 fourth rates, 132 frigates, and 86 sloops of war, besides many armed Indiamen, in all more than 426 ships of war; and have not the enemy, with scarce the vestige of a navy, taken nearly two thousand sail of merchantmen more from us than we have taken from them; and are these no proofs of the Minister's error, misconduct, wickedness, or incapacity?

Have we not a standing army of 300,000 men, and have we not more generals and other officers than all our allies and enemies together; and yet have not our troops been obliged to retreat from the field, and what remained alive to return home? Were there not seventy ships and five thousand men lost by the failures of the West-India expedition?—and have not the enemy, with a handful of adventurers, and without any regular force, ravaged and captured those distressed colonies, in despite of our generals, our immense expenditure, and our numerous and well-appointed naval equipments?

Has not the Minister connived at the perpetuation of the slavery of the unfortunate Africans, and thereby given them new incitements to rage, revenge, and destruction; and has he not brought over our philanthropic Mr. Wilberforce to assist him in his diabolical plan, and to go hand in hand with him in the enslaving and starving the people of this country?

MAGNA CHARTA.

In the reign of William Pitt has it not been forbidden by law to discuss the constitution of these realms; and has not the immaculate Minister dared any man to call gentlemen to account that are high in office? But I am in hopes that the noise of the grunting swinish multitude, and the roaring of John Bull, will awaken the understanding of the people, and convince

convince them that there is no defcription of men in any free country, who are not liable to be called to account for conftantly adding houfe to houfe, field to field, and fund to fund, with the produce of the public plunder.

NOOTKA-SOUND.

This was another project of our Minifter to enrich this country! This bufinefs is of too recent a date to need my entering into any particulars, more than that a Britifh merchant had been infulted by a haughty Don, prevented from fifhing in Nootka-Sound; for which, and fome other infults, damages were rated againft the Spaniard at twenty thoufand pounds. Mr. Pitt, on hearing this, tacks on the Manilla ranfom, and of courfe had a legal claim on the Spaniards for 3,020,000l. and how manfully he fupported his claim by warlike preparations. Exprefles were fent to and from Madrid, by meffengers as bufy as poor boys employed in fetching farthing candles; till at length 4,000,000l. was fpent in the purfuit, of courfe the demand was increafed to 7,020,000l. No doubt men of the beft abilities were employed in this important bufinefs; at length Mr. Pitt was fuccefsful, and for the honour of the country (not much to his own) damages were recovered to the amount of twenty thoufand pounds—fo that (including the Manilla ranfom, and the money fpent in the purfuit of recovering) Mr. Pitt's difappointment and the lofs to this country was only feven millions! ——We are not to forget that Mr. Pitt was fuccefsful; twenty thoufand pounds were received, and I believe the whole of this fum was fent by three different inftalments, and it was inferted at three different times in the Treafury papers that money was arrived in a fhip from Spain to pay the damages recovered againft the Spaniards at Nootka-Sound.

I wifh our heaven-born Minifter had read the hiftory of Oliver Cromwell. He fettled a fimilar infult insult received from the French, without a shilling expence to this country. An honest Quaker having been robbed of his ship and cargo at sea by a Frenchman, went to Oliver, and made his complaint, who ordered him to make out the estimate of his loss; which he did, and carried to the Protector. " Is this a just account?" said Oliver. ' Yes,' answered the Quaker. " Will you carry a letter for me to Paris?" ' Yes.' Which letter Oliver immediately wrote, and directed it to the minister at Paris, who was frequently waited on by the injured Quaker, but he could obtain no interview. After waiting at Paris till his patience was exhausted, he returned to England, and waited on the Protector. " Are you paid?" said Oliver. ' No,' answered the Quaker. The immediate consequence was, that an English frigate was ordered to sea, to take the first French ship he met met with that would be likely to pay the Quaker's expences. The business was soon done; the ship and cargo was brought into port and sold, the injured subject was paid, and the balance was sent to the French ambassador then in London, which he thought fit to receive, and the matter ended.

After all, I think Mr. Pitt must have read the history of Oliver Cromwell, and that he was well informed as to this circumstance; then what can he say for himself relative to the expenditure of four millions to recover twenty thousand pounds! But the times are now altered; it was then the swinish multitude were in the habit of enjoying the fruits of their labour—stock-jobbing and ministerial swindling had not then made their appearance.

BANK OF ENGLAND.

It is the general idea of the people of this country, that this Bank hath one and the same interest in support of national credit and national prosperity, but the facts will prove the very reverse; as no one circumstance can be proved so injurious to this country for monopolizing money. The extravagance of

Charles the Second, and the political intrigues of the Revolution in 1688, involved the government in expenditure to a confiderable amount beyond the public revenue of the ftate; and among the devices of that period for fupporting the meafures of the ruling party, was the inftitution of the Bank, commonly called the Bank of England. Before the reign of the Stuarts, the expences of the government rarely exceeded the annual income; on the acceffion of King William the practice of loans for the public exigencies commenced, the intereft of which was provided by annual taxes.

In July 1704 the Bank was incorporated by act of parliament, and empowered to receive fubfcriptions for 1,200,000l. upon which government agreed to pay 8l. per cent. per annum, befides 4000l. per annum for management, and here commenced the great evil of the prefent enormous funded debt; the whole of which would have been provided for prior to Mr. Pitt's funding, had government referved the profits of banking for the benefit of the public, but Mr. Pitt having exceeded all others to fuch an aftonifhing degree in the public expenditure, that no means could be devifed to fupport his extravagance. By feveral further advances to the Bank of England in 1709 and 1742, the capital of the Bank (that is, the fum that government ftood indebted to the corporation) was increafed to 3,200 000l. and the intereft reduced firft to fix, and on the 1ft of Auguft 1743 to three per cent. which has been ufually called the original ftock of the Bank By fubfequent financial operations at feveral periods to the prefent day, the Bank ftock or debt of government has augmented the capital to 11,686,800l. upon which fum the government pay intereft quarterly, but the dividends to the proprietors is made half-yearly. The profits of the Bank arife from the ufe of the public money, acting as private gentlemen's bankers, and to the Exchequer, receiving the proceeds

ceeds of all the public taxes from the several collectors, without any charge for the use thereof, and advancing when required the supposed amount of the land-tax, and other sums for the use of government, for which an allowance is made by government, exclusive of the annual allowance by charter, and the sum of 450l. per million for the management of the public funds. Which last sum, prior to Mr. Pitt's funding, amounts to the sum of 200,000l. annually, exclusive of 5,898l. 3s. 5d. for the management of their own capital; and will at the present day, or as soon as the money is funded that hath been spent by Mr. Pitt, amount to the sum of 300,000l. annually, for management alone. The use of unclaimed dividends is a resource of vast profit. Government pays the Bank for their circulation of exchequer bills, and agency or commission for receiving subscriptions for their public loans. The profits of the Bank in the early part of their institution were very considerable for their trade in bullion, and the discounting of private bills; which they have been able to carry on to great extent and the utmost advantage, by the capitals of those who lodge their property in the Bank as a place of security, and for which they pay no interest. But the great and incalculable riches of the Bank arises from its notes forming the principal medium of its circulation in the capital to an immense amount, and considerably throughout the kingdom; and it is not to be forgotten, that in all issues of whatever kind to government or individuals, that paper forms the most considerable part of the issues, and the profits paid for the use and loans of money, is equally derived by the Bank for the use of that paper.

Of this species of profit an example may be satisfactory here, though it is stated before in this work; and as the financial capacity of the present Minister hath been extolled, among his other heaven-born qualities, the following contract of his in 1785, after three years of peace, and when the French Revolution had not formed a ladder for his wild ambition.

	L.	s.	d.
Amount of Bills funded 2d of March 1786, at 5 per cent.	9,865.941	18	4
Capital created -	10,990,651	10	4
Profit by a fingle Contract	1,124,709	12	0

being the amount of a bonus to the Bank for a peace loan, exclufive of 5l. per cent. per annum for interelt on the amount of the grofs capital.

From the above general account of the Bank of England, it appears that its credit is eftablifhed on the fecurity of the government, and that its ftability mult be the fame. It appears alfo, that its ftock is the capital of the public debt created by government, by various contracts with the proprietors of the Bank, and the Bank holds the exclufive privilege of public banking, befides various immenfe allowances for employing that capital. They trade for their own felect advantage; and the inftitution exhibits this peculiarity, that with thefe privileges and profits the capital of the Bank alone is accountable for its debts; and the property of thofe who compofe the body of Bank Proprietors is not refponfible for any deficiency that may arife from any fudden failure of its funds, or from any circumftance whatever.

Adam Smith, in his Wealth of Nations, fays the Bank of England cannot hurt their creditors till they have loft the whole of their capital of 11,800,000l. If they have lent their fecurities for 100,000,000l. on a rotten foundation, and on the fupport only of the above 11,800,000l. what have they done but loft it? Quere, How are they reimburfed the immenfe fecurities that they have given? By nothing more than the profits of the labours of the people, for which no proof can be found of its ftability; nor even is it the will of the people to part with that proportion of their earnings which they have been accuftomed to do. It may be argued alfo, that the land-tax is bound; but they can have no aid from that quarter, as the whole

whole produce does not amount to two millions annually, therefore is not sufficient to support his Majesty's civil list, with Mr. Pitt and his friends.

We will now suppose, for example, that a mercantile or any trading house had begun a business with 11,800l. and obtained a credit of 100,000l. and entrusted insolvent people, that could make but a miserable dividend; what then must be the situation of their creditors, unless they could obtain an act of parliament to pay them in paper? What dividend could be expected from the Bank of England paper, supposing their notes were sent in rapidly upon them? Are we to suppose that the nation is 200,000,000l. the richer, because Mr. Pitt hath spent so much? No—but to a certainty from ten to twelve millions the poorer, he having sent so much specie out of the kingdom. What security then can the Bank of England have received for the immense paper medium, but a mortgage of the profits of the labour of the people?

It appears a most extraordinary circumstance, what they can have done with their immense profits; as we have no public information of their having divided more of late than from eight to nine, or at the very utmost, ten per cent. when their profits, if fairly estimated from the following circumstance, cannot be less than forty per cent. For example, their profits for one day have amounted to 1,124,907l; annual profit by stock-jobbing not less than 1,000,000l. interest on the capital (for which they pay no interest themselves) 500,000l.; interest by government securities for the loan of their circulating notes, at least 70,000,000l. which must produce them at least a profit annually of 3,500,000l.; for the management of the public debt, 300,000l.; besides the profits of unclaimed dividends, and notes lost, that of course never return into their Bank for payment. Certainly they cannot have increased their capital without the consent

sent of parliament; then what account can be given for what they have done with their astonishing profits, when it never has appeared openly that they have divided more than ten per cent. and their profits appear to be more than forty per cent. per annum. They have lent all their capital and their securities, (together not less than one hundred millions) for which government has secured to them the profits of the labour of the people; and they have hitherto received the full interest, even before it was due.

Admitting there were one million of working people, and each man earned ten shillings per week by his labour, which certainly is the utmost extent, allowing for holidays, the whole amount of their labour could not be more than twenty-five millions annually; and of this, in time of peace, fifteen millions will be swallowed up to pay interest of money. A principal part of this sum is divided among Bank Directors, a set of men who cannot prove of the least utility, further than at a time of public corruption for filling seats in parliament. They can talk of a few thousands with as much indifference as of a few half-pence. So much for the balance of corruption being in favour of men who formerly thought it an honour to serve their country without fee or reward. To the above must be added at least from three to four millions annually for navy, army, placemen, pensioners, and stock-jobbers, who are in the habits of receiving unlimited profits.

In the present case it appears clearly, that from these circumstances, and the increased price of the necessaries of life, the people have not more than the last farthing out of their penny. This will be proved by the difference in the price of the necessaries of life, within the memory of the author; and this is the only security Mr. Pitt can give to pay the interest of his additional securities, and on which he is ready to receive another hundred millions of paper circulating medium,

medium, if the people should be fools enough to continue the war to gratify his ambition. However this influx of paper circulation is the riches that Mr. Pitt hath so much boasted of, as having exceeded that of all other nations in the world; and truly there is nothing more wanted to add stability. But what hath our heaven-born Minister done, but mistook the shadow for the substance, and sent nearly one half of the real specie out of the kingdom;—does not this conduct in finance demand an immediate reform? And what have the Bank of England done, but lost their capital, by suffering it to be sent out of the kingdom? This could not be done without their consent, and with mercenary views of increasing the value of their paper circulation.

Our heaven-born Minister tells us, that our merchandize, exports, and imports, exceeds all other nations in Europe or the world. But what does he allude to? What are the most considerable of our importations? Saltpetre, brimstone, and other naval stores, for fitting out ships, manufactures, soldiers' clothes, swords, firelocks, and great guns; which, if carried on for a thousand years, will never add a shilling to the riches of the kingdom, or a bit of bread—these are the advantages of a heaven-born Minister. If we give him credit for a balance of the conquest of the Cape, and the Dutch men of war taken, it will not pay a penny in the pound on the money spent by himself; and then we are at a loss to make up for two thousand of our merchant ships taken by the enemy over and above the number we have taken from them.

PAPER CIRCULATING MEDIUM.

I am far from thinking the trade of this country could be carried on without paper circulation, but who then is the best entitled to the advantages arising from it but the public, who will take such kind of payments instead of cash? If a proper use had been made of the increase of paper circulation, well secured

by

by an honest government, it would have answered the purpose so far as to have saved at least twelve hundred thousand pounds annually; which is sent out of the kingdom to pay the Dutch and other foreigners, for the interest of the stock they hold in our funds, in addition to the advantages they take by buying in when our funds are low, and selling out when they are high. In the year 1792 it was said the Dutch sold out of our funds to such an amount as produced them a profit of upwards of six hundred thousand pounds; this was a sum that never could be reimbursed to this country, and of course, with all other sums craftily purloined from the inhabitants of this country by stock-jobbing, must be made up by taxes. That the price of the necessaries of life must be increased by taxation, is so clear a case, that I almost think it needless to produce any proofs; but for the information of the few that may not be so well satisfied as to the fact, I will state Soame Jenyns's judicious remarks on taxation, published 1767.

' *Thoughts on the causes and consequences of the present High Price of Provisions, by Soame Jenyns.*

' Every new tax does not only affect the price of the commodity on which it is laid, but that of all others, whether it be taxed or not; and with which at first sight, it seems to have no manner of connexion. Thus, for instance, a tax on candles must rise the price of a coat or a pair of breeches; because out of these all the taxes on the candles of the woolcomber, the weaver, with a number of others in the woollen branch, the taylor must likewise be paid in proportion. A duty on ale must rise the price of shoes; because from all the taxes upon ale drank by the tanner, leather-dresser, and shoemaker, (which is not a little) must be refunded. No tax is immediately laid upon corn, but the price of it must necessarily advance, because out of all the innumerable taxes paid by the farmer on windows, soap, candles, malt,

malt, hops, leather falt, and a thoufand others, muft be repaid; fo that corn is as much taxed, as if a duty by the bufhel had been laid upon it. For taxes are like the various ftreams that form an inundation by feparate channels; they feparately find admiffion, and unite at laft, and overwhelm the whole. The man, therefore, who fold fand upon the afs, and raifed the price of it during the late war, though abufed for an mpofition, moft certainly acted upon right reafon; for though there were then no taxes impofed upon the fand or affes, yet he found by experience, that from the taxes laid on almoft all other things, he could not maintain himfelf, his wife, or his afs, as cheap as formerly; he was therefore under the neceffity of advancing the price of the fand, out of which alone the taxes he paid muft be refunded.'

Taxes created to fupport the credit of paper coinage is a circumftance that no more proves the wealth of the country, than the rich equipage of the Lord Mayor of London; or that becaufe the firft magiftrate of the capital can afford to give a dinner at an expence of five thoufand pounds, from the profits of fmall bread, poverty and wretchednefs are unknown in his jurifdiction. Palaces may lift their heads, velvet may fpread to the bafis of the mountains, but it is in the humble cottage and the furrowed fields, among the bufy hum of men, that profperity is to be recognized.

The indifference or intereftednefs of men, and the perplexed and improvident conduct of the financial adminiftration, muft naturally lay out of the immediate addrefs of perfons who do not beftow much labour and time on the ftudy of a dry fubject; which I mean to prove by the fhort reafoning of men in other refpects poffeffing the firft abilities. I confider that Oppofition as well as the Treafury have their paragraph writers; though I fuppofe the latter may have fix to one in their favour, and their hirelings have their own terms to make.

As

As I profess myself to be a well-informed man respecting the important business of finance, I applied to one of the proprietors of a morning paper, in hopes to be introduced to a high character in opposition.— The nature of my business was enquired into, which I answered; and the reply to me was, that no information of that sort could be useful either to Mr. Fox or Mr. Sheridan, for that they were both the first calculators in the world. But to prove the mistake of this gentleman, I shall not only take some extracts from a morning paper, but likewise some parts of the speeches of those gentlemen who were said to have such excellence as calculators and financiers; and clearly prove their short reasoning on these important objects—to which we may partly attribute the great length Mr. Pitt hath run in the destruction of the credit of this country; in fact, he hath completed it, for it will bear no more paper circulating medium.

From the Morning Chronicle, April 9th, 1796:—
'The charter of the Bank of England has still eleven years to run, and those eleven years of monopoly are as much their estate, as any private property in England; to incroach upon it in any way, would be such a violation of faith as would be the death blow to our credit as a nation. We are not ignorant of Mr. Pitt's partiality to innovation; he abhors the beaten track, as unworthy of a genius so inventive; but let him practise his experiments in any thing but finance. There is but one means of preserving the credit of a nation and an individual, and it is become an English maxim to be open and fair in your dealings.'

From the Morning Chronicle, Oct. 15, 1796:—
'At length Mr. Boyd's committee for circulating medium have digested their plan, and it is regularly to be proposed to the Minister, and if they gain his consent, to parliament. The outlines of it is that the Corporation of the Bank of England shall be permitted to increase their capital 2,000,000l. each proprietor

prietor having leave to subscribe the sum in proportion to his present stock, and which he will be eager to do, we suppose, on account of the advantage it will present to him; and from the enlarged capital it is expected they shall increase their advantage in favour of trade. Whether the Committee mean to demand from Mr. Pitt, in order to give efficiency to this measure, that he shall not drain the Bank, or inundate the market with paper, we know not; but it is certain without some restraint upon Ministers of this kind, or without a change of Ministry all these expedients will only be to furnish him with new resources to go on in a wasteful expence without estimate. Nor is it merely that his new system opens the door to uncontrouled dissipation, but it disappoints the very end which this committee has in view; for how can trade expect to borrow money at 5l. per cent. when the Minister makes the nation pay 15l.? The Bank may be liberal, and we believe they have been so; but it is obvious, that all the aid they give is swallowed up in navy bills, and every spirit of commercial enterprize checked, except the contracts for the state, where the discounts are added to the price of the commodity.'

From the Morning Herald, Oct. 22, 1796.

'COMMERCIAL REGULATION.

'A committee of merchants, we are informed, waited upon the Chancellor of the Exchequer and the Directors of the Bank, regarding the want of an increased quantity of circulating medium to aid the commercial concerns of the kingdom. The following plans have been proposed, viz. That the navy and victualling bills, and other floating paper, be funded immediately; that the Bank increase their capital two millions, and issue six millions extraordinary in discounting fair mercantile bills; that any person may mortgage to the Bank, estates, public funds, and any solid securities, and during the existence of such mortgage shall have fair mercantile bills discounted

discounted to such amount, over and above the usual sum employed by the Bank in discount; that the bankers of London, Westminster, and parts adjacent, shall be authorized by parliament to form a company for a limited time, and in consequence of each mortgaging to the body of bankers solid property, each shall issue notes of that firm to such amount, in discount of fair mercantile bills, and that such shall for a limited time be deemed in law good and proper payment of any kind or sort whatsoever.'

From Mr. Pitt's speech in the House of Commons, 29th October, 1796.——The Chancellor of the Exchequer rose to make the motion that a proposal had been made at a meeting of the merchants and bill holders two days ago, when the 3 per cents. were at 58l. the 4 per cents. at 75l. and the 5 per cents. at 88l. The nature of the proposals was, that all navy, victualling, and transport bills, which were dated August, September, and October, should be funded in the 3 per cents. at one half below the price of stock upon the day when the proposal was made; the 4 per cents. at $73\frac{1}{2}$l. and the 5 per cents. at $85\frac{1}{2}$l. He would not trouble the committee by going through a particular statement of the difference of the bonus, but it was somewhat higher than in proportion to the difference in the funds; the average price was a bonus of $1\frac{1}{4}$ on the 3 per cents. $1\frac{1}{4}$ on the 4 per cents and $2\frac{1}{4}$ on the 5 per cents. Besides these, he had provided for 2,500,000l. exchequer bills, by allowing them to fund in the 3 per cents. at 56l. 10s. The committee was to observe his plan was to relieve the public credit, and give a free circulation of money.

Mr. Hussey remarked, that navy and transport bills had been always considered as so much ready money given; the discount on them was from 14l. to 15l. per cent. Now if we look into and take the 3 per cent. consols at $57\frac{1}{2}$l. the loss to the public would be 6l. 2s. If they were invested in the 5 per cents.

cents, Mr. H. hoped the Minifter would ftate what the public were to pay for thefe twelve millions.

The Chancellor declared that Mr. Huffey had taken him on unfair ground, taking the rate of difcount as if the whole had accrued a difcount. He lamented that any of them fhould be at fo high a rate of intereft. In future it would be defirable to adopt fome method to avoid the accruing of fuch intereft; but fince it was done, it muft now be paid. It was not right to injure the original plan on which thefe bills were iffued; but what plan would produce the moft advantageous confequences to the public? Mr. Huffey wifhes to know what the average price the Chancellor now propofed would coft the public. Mr. Huffey fays, that fuch navy bill holders as obtained them at 14l. per cent. difcount would fund their money at 49l. nearly nothing but paper being advanced. What he complained of was, that fuch a debt had been incurred, without provifion being made for the payment of it, fo that a lofs fo very confiderable to the public might not have happened.

Mr. Fox's remarks on Mr. Pitt fays, that he faps the flourifhing fituation of the country. Mr. Fox fays that it was impoffible for every gentleman, whether in or out of Parliament, not to fix their attention to the general fituation of the country, which, fince the late regulations, had produced fuch enormous difcounts on navy bills as 14l. or 15l. per cent. Mr. Fox then proceeded to animadvert on the different claffes of the bills, according to the propofed regulation and agreements; and obferved, that with regard to thofe bills which would become payable on the 12th of December, and which might be funded in the 5l. per cents, that, befides the intereft accruing, they would receive 100l. capital for what was worth about 86l. the difcount to which being added, it appears they would receive for that fhort period a bonus of 6l, 1cs. which, upon the whole, he calculated

lated would amount to the enormous intereſt of 103l. per cent. per annum.

I cannot follow Mr. Fox, as I do not know the time the bills had to run. It is ſufficient to ſay the country had got into ſuch a ſituation. Parliament had no right to force the bill-holders to any other terms than they themſelves approved of. Mr. Fox declared that, for one, he was much inclined to enquire how the country came into ſuch a ſituation. He acknowledged the nature of the debt was changed by funding from 4l. per cent. to 5l. 18s. per cent. circulating medium. *Morning Chronicle,* 31 *October,* 1796.

Mr. Pitt has at laſt condeſcended to attempt an explanation of his novel and extraordinary propoſition, that our national proſperity is the real cauſe of our national embarraſſment, or, as he more minutely explains it, that the national wealth, owing to the late rapid increaſe, has become ſo, that there exiſt not in the country means of circulating it; the ſharks have ſwallowed ſo many of the ſmall fiſh, that they cannot digeſt them, and yet are wanting more; and this deficiency in our circulating medium is the cauſe of our preſent difficulties. Of this ſuppoſed increaſe of riches he ſtated two proofs; firſt, the flouriſhing ſtate of our revenue, ſecondly, the extent of our commerce, and conſequent opulence of our merchants. That the reader may have an accurate view of the ratio in which our revenue denotes, by the increaſe, the augmentation of our capital, we extract from the papers before Parliament the annual produce of the old taxes ſince the year 1792.

From 1792 to 1793	£. 14,284,295
1793 to 1794	13,813,290
1794 to 1795	13,674,892
1795 to 1796	13,138,727
1796 — 1797	12,798,327

With respect to the prosperity of our commerce, and the extended opulence of our merchants, if we are rightly informed concerning the contents of the addresses to his Majesty's privy council from the merchants from Exeter, and other places, the energy of their complaints creates a very different impression; but indeed we know of no extension of any branch of our commerce, except that which is carried on in Change-Alley, and occasioned by Mr. Pitt's increased and increasing manufacture of three, four, and five per cents. navy, victualling, transport, treasury, and exchequer bills.

Can he really be so blind, as not to see in this the real source of our calamities and embarassments? Can he be ignorant that this derangement in the natural order of our expences, is the obvious causes of our difficulties; that the circulating medium drawn from the natural implements, the circulation of raw materials and manufactures, and engrossed by the forced circulation of the securities he has thrown into the market, is the foundation of the scarcity of which he complains? This is a calamity that must daily increase our difficulties, and accelerate the diminution of our riches, for there is no parallel to be drawn from the circulation of other commodities to that of omnium or exchequer bills. Where a manufacturer has a quick sale for his goods to the merchant, the merchant to the shopkeeper, and the shopkeeper to the customer, this enlivens industry, gives new encouragement to the first dealer, and makes him produce more and better commodities of the same species; but what are the productions we owe to Change Alley, or even what consumption, except that of coffee, pens, ink, and paper, we have not yet learned.

'We have often experienced Mr. Pitt's presumptuous confidence in his talents of persuasion, but we cannot believe that even he fancies that by a few vapouring sentences he can have persuaded any order of

men

men that the capital of the country has increased in its riches of late. Will the stockholder who recollects in his books a capital in the 3 per cents, amounting to 96,000l. and now sees it reduced in a few years to 58,000l. become with ease a proselyte to this new doctrine; or can any man believe it, who looks at the following plain statement of the diminution of one branch of our capital? Hence comes the calculations in which the writer says he proves a loss of 90,647,648l. As to the statement of figures proving the difference, no doubt but the writer is right; but it is not an object of consequence enough to examine, as he is totally wrong in his reasons on the subject, which I mean to prove in a future page.

'Again,' says the writer, ' It is to us a more serious object of regret than so strong a proof of the diminution of our national wealth, at such a moment to have a minister of finance so ignorant and uninformed as not to be ashamed of having recourse to such an old refuted subterfuge as this paradox about his circulating medium. Did the compass of our paper permit, we could trace the pretence to the mouth of every adventurer in finance, from the time of Law to the present moment, and we could refute it in such a manner as to exhibit to the public in a strong and lamentable point of view the folly of those who have now brought it forward; consistent however, with the narrow limits in which we are forced to treat the question, we cannot do it more justice than by quoting the following passage from a work long ago published by one of the most celebrated writers on political œconomy.' This quotation being in the French language, it would be but a stumbling-block to nineteen readers out of twenty, or even the readers of newspapers; but to continue the plain English, the writer says: 'We have dwelt so long on his ministerial whim, because there are many who begin to think, that as Mr. Pitt despairs after his numerous experiments of augmenting the circulating medium, so as to render it adequate to the proper distribution of the supposed increased riches of the country, he has it in contemplation to restore the proportion by a judicious diminution of the capital; and that as the last confiding parliament added 100 millions to our debt to support the minister's old prejudices, the confidence of the present will be exerted to a similar extent in maintaining his new conceits; so that the nation have ultimately to regret, that betwixt the complimentary sacrifices of their representatives to the minister's aversion to practical experiments abroad, and the love of new theory at home, it positively will be loaded with an additional payment of 10,000,000l.'— Quere, I suppose he meant annually.

'We have said, that the most lavish bargain ever Mr. Pitt made, from the first moment that he commenced his career in finance, by conciliating the money-lenders in 1784 in the funding of navy bills, came infinitely short of the job with which he is now striving to make his court to the directors of public corporations, and other capitalists in the city. Not to fatigue our readers with long calculations, we will put it into a short and perspicuous point of view. In September last a person for 85l. bought a navy bill of 100l. and for this bill with its interest up to the 12th of December, he is to receive in the 3 per cents. for ever -   -   £.175 15 0

Suppose he had bought in the 3 per cent. consols, taking them at the same time, his 85l. would have produced him only   -   147 15 0

Bonus to the holder of navy bills on 85l. for three months   £.28 0 0

It is certain that this bonus does not apply to all the four classes, but the average of the discount for the last seven months is somewhat above 9¼ per cent. from the following prices:

In

In April the discount was 5¾
May — 4¼
June — 6¼
July — 8½
August — 11½
September 15
October 13

Now taking the amount of navy bills to be issued at that time to be 7,000,000l. only, the discount alone to be shared amongst the holders, will form an addition to the capital of our debt, besides the interest of 4l. per cent. up to the 12th of December of 600.00 l. which converted into 3 per cents. at 57l. (which is also the average) will form a capital with the interest of more than one million, and this is the transaction of seven months only. The objections of Mr. Boyd to funding the navy only until the 15th of December, had their force with the minister; and the public thus pay an additional interest from the 18th of October to the 12th of December next of 70,00 l. on twelve millions of navy, making a capital of 120,000l. in the 3 per cent. consols for ever. The fact is, that what is funded in the 3 per cents. bears interest from July last, and the navy holder receives interest on his bills till the 12th of December next; so that they receive, and the public pay a double interest.

It is a curious and remarkable fact that the navy debt, through the whole American war, up to the year 1782, amounted only to the sum of 11,318,450l. and we find that Mr. Pitt's navy debt amounts in one year to 11,93,167l. 19s. 6d.; so that in one year Mr. Pitt squandered above six hundred thousand pounds more than Lord North spent in seven years. Yet this is the œconomical minister, of whom Mr. Burke says, that ' if ever the finances of this nation can be retrieved, Mr. Pitt is the man to retrieve them.' We knew not how Mr. Burke had made up his

his mind to this affertion, until Simkin, in his poetical verfion of the pamphlet, folved the difficulty:

"Indeed, fays friend Simkin, if there liveth a man
"Of talents fufficient, our Minifter can;
"Provided his powers of faving and mending
"Correfpond with his powers of deftroying and fpending."

The foregoing extracts are taken in order to prove the weak reafoning of Oppofition to the minifter's meafures refpecting finance, and the folly of wifhing their leader to be at the head of that precipice, where the foundation is fo narrow and rotten as to be expected every moment to tumble into a Pitt? What then can be done by Mr. Fox, or any other minifter, without an entire new fyftem of finance?

The editor of the Morning Chronicle of the 16th of April 1796, tells us that 'the Bank of England has eleven years to come of their charter, and that the leaft incroachment on it would be the death-blow to our credit as a nation.' Indeed he might as well have talked of giving the death-blow to a man, by firing a fhot through his head, feven years after he had been nailed up in his coffin. When the Bank of England commenced contracts that were ufurious and extortionate, it was then that the death-blow was ftruck to the nation's and their own credit.

In the next inftance, he blames Mr. Pitt for not following the beaten track. Though it is true that any track was better than Mr. Pitt's, yet what would have been the difference in following the old beaten track? The deftruction of the national credit, to which we are now arrived, would have taken a little more time. I recommend the writer to look into the Commiffioners' Accounts, publifhed in the year 1786, and my remarks on the fame fubject, in the Guardian of Public Credit, publifhed in 1788, and he will there fee what deftruction was made on the national credit by the Bank, by purfuing the old beaten track.

He

He remarks in the same paragraph, that there is but one way of preserving the credit of a nation and that of an individual. Does he not know what care an established law of the land has taken to protect and save the individual, by severe penalties on usury and extortion? yet he does not think the public entitled to the benefit of those laws; the destruction was effected for the want of it.

Again, the 15th of October 1796, he says 'the Bank of England shall be permitted to increase their capital two millions.' As the cry from this bulwark of national credit, and all the opulent bankers, is the want of cash, how is this addition to take place, but by a new coinage of two millions worth of paper?— Again, he says, 'No doubt but they will readily come into it, on account of the advantages; the proprietors are each to have a share, in proportion to their present stock.' Admitting this addition of stock to take place by paper coinage, and the stock worth 150l. per cent. the subscribers immediately increase their own fortunes one million in consequence of this new coinage of paper being added to their capital. The writer wishes to know whether Mr. Pitt wants to inundate the market with paper. What market can he mean—a pig-market, or paper-market? as there can be no money-market without cash. Can he be so blind as not to see there is no such thing as money for the market he speaks of? This market differs as much from a money-market, as a market of fine new linen would from a market of rags; but if parliament will continue to vote such supplies, how is the minister to go on with the accursed business of the war, but with additional paper coinage?

Surely it is wrong for Mr. Fox's friends to advise him to take upon himself the management of the finances of the country on its present foundation, to ease Mr. Pitt of a burthen of which the country can never be relieved without an entire new system. Most assuredly furedly Mr. Fox had better be any thing than Chancellor of the Exchequer, on the prefent infupportable foundation. His friends muft be infane to perfuade him to it, as no doubt but the rotten fabric muft foon give way, without an entire new fyftem; as the circulating cafh will not be fufficient to pay the extended army and navy that is now propofed; and though Mr. Fox was not the original inftrument or caufe of the approaching difafter, he had better be any thing than Chancellor of the Exchequer.

The paragraph writer gives Mr. Boyd credit for having in his views the relief of trade. Let him look at Mr. Boyd's conduct refpecting contracts for loans, and compare with his own opinion refpecting Mr. Boyd's views, and he will find himfelf a fhort reafoner; and when he faid the minifter makes the public pay 15 per cent. if he had included principal and intereft, he might have as well faid 50 per cent.— ' The Bank of England (he fays) may have been liberal, and we believe they have been fo;' but before he had ventured on this affertion, he fhould have looked into the Commiffioners' Accounts publifhed in 1786, and my remarks in the Guardian of Public Credit, publifhed in 1788, and I have no doubt but he would have formed a better judgment of their liberality.

Is it poffible that Mr. Fox or his friends could be fo fhort-fighted, as to fuppofe he could be fupported by all the aid he could obtain from the Bank of England? I wifh them to be convinced;—and fuppofe the Bank of England to have a run of a fhilling in the pound on all their notes in circulation, we fhould find that not only their own coffers would be drained, but every drawer through Lombard-ftreet, the city, and environs—even Mr. Boyd, the contractor for waggon loads of guineas. How can it be otherwife, when we know that a capital of cafh of ten millions, the utmoft that hath been in circulation for any one time, hath accumulated to five hundred millions of ftock.

Mr. Fox, suppoſing he takes the lead in financeering, has a debt of five hundred millions to provide for, which has burthened the labours of the people to the very utmoſt, and will want new funding, to pay the intereſt every year. How then is it poſſible that he or any other miniſter can go on, without a radical reform in finance? The whole of the land in the kingdom is worth no more than five hundred millions. Taking the annual land-tax at an average of two millions, and the average per cent. at two ſhillings in the pound, at twenty-five years purchaſe, it is worth no more than five hundred millions. The two millions annual land-tax is not ſufficient to pay his Majeſty's civil liſt, and Mr. Pitt and his friends. The whole burthen of annual intereſt, amounting to fifteen millions, muſt come out of the profits of trade, and the labour of the people; of which the preſent taxes ſwallow up three farthings out of every penny, nine pence out of every ſhilling, and fifteen ſhillings out of every pound; ſo that the labouring people are now ſtarving on the produce of the fourth and laſt farthing. Yet on the credit of this Mr. Pitt is attempting to make new mortgages to an aſtoniſhing amount, and conſiderable new funding muſt take place every year in a peace eſtabliſhment, to pay arrears of intereſt for ſums unprovided for, and nothing to increaſe the revenue, but paper coinage.

What a Don Quixote windmill-fighting piece of buſineſs has Mr. Fox to engage in! Let them conſider but for a moment, and they muſt ſee that nothing can be done to ſupport the credit of the country, but a new ſyſtem of finance, a compromiſe between debtor and creditor, and an annihilation of the ſwindling practice of ſtock-jobbing. But how does Mr. Fox treat the ſubject, I mean the circumſtance of Mr. Pitt's having added near two hundred millions?— Juſt as though the creditor had lain down guineas for theſe enormous contracts. It is aſtoniſhing that

the

the very idea should be imposed on the public; not ten millions of specie could have gone through the hands of the loan-monger in any one year, notwithstanding all this, twenty millions are contracted for, and another twenty millions in another six months, if called upon by the minister; and no doubt, if the paper-market was not so glutted, twenty millions might be brought forward every month. For this straw-like security the people have an extravagant interest to pay, and if Mr. Pitt could possibly screw so much out of the people, from 50l. to 100l. per cent. premium, witness his conduct, as money borrowed by himself in the year 1785 produced no more at the rate of 3 per cent. than 55l. a profit of 70l. on 100l. sterling, as has been fairly proved in this work.

As I pledged myself to the public that this should not be a party pamphlet, I have again to charge Mr. Fox and his friends for short reasoning on this important business, I mean the support of national credit;— I am sorry to find too much reason to doubt their sincerity. Did Mr. Fox or his friends ever complain that the fluctuating money funding system was a bad one, or did they ever enter into the merits of this important business, so as to prove that the involvement of the nation respecting its extravagant debt prior to Mr. Pitt's funding, was occasioned by extortionate and usurious contracts; and that the Commissioners' Accounts in the year 1786 proves a debt contracted for the public in long annuities to the amount of 1,193,674l. 7s. 3d. This sum is to be paid annually, the principal part of it from 70 to 98 years, and for which the Commissioners say that no money was ever received? Did they ever complain of near 200,000l. being paid annually to the Bank of England for management, and that the said charge for management is now increased to 300,000l. though the same business might be done and handsomely paid for at the expence of 15,000l. and the sums or saving, including the above 1,193,674l. 7s. 3d. with its compound interest, prior to Mr. Pitt's funding, would have been sufficient to have discharged the whole of the then principal debt in the course of forty-three years, and without an additional shilling in new taxes. Did Mr. Fox or his friends ever complain of Mr. Pitt's first usurious contract with the Bank of England, that securities were given by Mr. Pitt in the 5 per cents. for 1,124,709l. 12s. as a douceur, and for which neither money nor paper was received? Did they ever complain that six millions had been wasted of the public money by Mr. Pitt, from the year 1786 to the year 1794, in order to continue the deception of lessening the funded debt; and that if the rotten fabrick of national credit could be supported, eighty millions must be paid on a debt funded by Mr. Pitt, for which no money had been received? Did he ever complain of Mr. Pitt's subterfuge in changing the nature of the Emperor's loan in that new-fangled form that it would produce no more than 4ll. 10s. 8d. per cent. when converted into the 3 per cents. which were then at 63l. making a douceur of 50l. per cent. to the subscribers; and that if ever it was intended the Emperor should pay, would not the nature and enormity of the contract be a sufficient reason for his refusing to pay? for if he had the benefit of our own laws, he certainly would be justified in refusing to pay.

The terms of the two loans, when connected together, produced a profit of 14l. 11s. Provided the stock had been sold at the price of the day, the total profits would have amounted to considerably more than three millions sterling; but our cunning man, in order to make the loan more palatable for this country, allows the subscribers to the Emperor's loan for every 100l. in the 3 per cents. 83l. 6s. 8d. and an annuity of 5l. per annum for 25 years, profits by interest bearing date before the subscriptions were completed 6l. by commission and discount 4l. so that no more than 90l. per cent.

cent. could be received into the exchequer. It hath been proved in page 24, that if the whole of the contract for the Emperor's loan had been converted into the 3 per cents. no more than 41l. 10s. 8d. was received in lieu of the securities for 100l. in the 3 per cents. Quere, then, what securities must have been given in our 3 per cents. to raise 100l. for the Emperor?

	L.	S.	D.		L.	S.
For	41	10	8	3 per cents.	100	0
For	41	10	8	Ditto	100	0
For	16	18	8	Ditto	40	17
	100	0	0		240	17

So that a subscriber for 100l. in the Emperor's loan obtained securities in our 3 per cents. to the amount of 240l. 17s.

Total amount of securities in the 3 per cents. given by this country to raise 4,800,000l. for the Emperor:

L.	S.	L.
100	0	4,800,000
100	0	4,800,000
40	17	1,960,000
240	17	11,560,000

proportion of securities in our 3 per cents. and for which this country is bound to pay, in order to obtain 4,800,000l. for the Emperor. Most assuredly an appeal to our own laws would exonerate the Emperor from ever paying a shilling. But what cares the loan-monger and stockjobber, when he thinks he has got John Bull by the horns to this extravagant swindling business? Have Opposition ever entered into the merits of the business, or even complained?

Mr. Burke endeavours to support these practices, by saying that 'if ever the finances of this nation can be retrieved, Mr. Pitt is the man to retrieve them.' It

is

is a pity that Mr. Burke's friends do not perſuade him to ſtop writing, unleſs he believed his own aſſertions, or could perſuade any body elſe to believe them. This Mr. Burke is the man that ſpoke and wrote ſo brilliantly in the praiſe of religion; what a pity he ſhould, at the decline of life, have bartered his opinion for the ſake of the additional luxury he may have probably to enjoy for a few years.

Oppoſition have omitted to notice that a capital of fifteen millions of ſpecie hath acquired mortgages on the profits of induſtry to the amount of five hundred millions, and chiefly by ſhuffling paper from hand to hand; of this bonus we may charge the Bank of England with a profit of four millions annually, for notes they have in circulation. No notice of this has been taken by Oppoſition. After all this what a poor proſpect muſt we have of their ſincerity!

I have an inſtance to produce of penalties on uſury and extortion in individual caſes. I lived in a neighbourhood in the weſt of England where a man began buſineſs in the ſale of grutts and ſalt, with a capital of one thouſand pounds; with his ſurplus profits he lent his diſtreſſed neighbours on uſurious contracts, which ſoon increaſed his capital to an incredible amount, and of courſe brought his diſtreſſed neighbours to a ſtate of beggary. An inſtance and a proof of his uſury came acroſs me, and I immediately commenced an action on the ſtatute, and recovered damages. The late Judge Nares, who tried the cauſe, (a gentleman as much famed for rectitude as any other man in his high ſtation) addreſſed the ſpecial jury nearly in the following words:—'Gentlemen, I conſider the ſubject before us as of the utmoſt importance to the moſt opulent and trading part of this great commercial country. You are not to conſider the trifling amount of the uſury, but that it is opening a field for the indulgence of avarice, which would be likely to know no bounds. In the natural courſe of

buſineſs

business there are frequently men that have a solid property, but it is not always in their power to turn their merchandize into cash; of course, necessity drives him to the monied man, and he must be supplied. If this man was left to the mercy of the usurer, the production of all his toil would be swallowed up, and in a short time the whole of his property together; and notwithstanding industry, and even penury, the industrious man must become a poor man. But the wisdom of the legislature hath thought fit to step in, and lay such restraints between the monied man, the merchant, and the tradesman, that each shall have a reasonable share in the profits.'

How reverse hath been the conduct of our leaders, between public debtor and creditor; by their injudicious conduct, during the whole of the present reign in particular, the kingdom is absolutely ruined, on account of no regard being paid to the salutary laws against usury and extortion. What can a profligate Administration say in their own defence? or what can Opposition say, to vindicate their short reasoning on so important a business?

When the present King came to the crown the following was the amount of the debt and annual interest: Total of the debt 75,137,926l. 14s. 2d. Annual interest 2,419,313l. 17s. 10d. By the time the whole of Mr. Pitt's incumbrances are brought in, the debt will be increased at least to 500,000,000l. bearing an annual interest of 15,000,000l. and upwards; so that a capital increase of the principal has taken place of considerably more than 400,000,000l. and an increase in interest of considerably more than 12,000,000l. Can we be surprized at the increased price of all the necessaries of life? 20,240,000l. was funded in the second year of the present reign; how much of this debt was contracted before the present reign I do not know, but this I do know, that the capital debt hath been increased more than four hundred

hundred millions, and the annual intereſt more than twelve millions, and all in the reign of the 'beſt of 'kings.' Since William the Conqueror we have had thirty-three crowned heads, twenty-nine of whom were males; and what a happineſs it was the former twenty-eight were not all 'the beſt of kings!' Sir Robert Walpole was pretty right, when he ſaid the nation would not bear a greater burthen than one hundred millions, for it was really the faɛt, provided the paper circulating medium had not increaſed ſo rapidly.

TRADING COMPANIES, 1795.
DIRECTORS OF THE BANK OF ENGLAND.

Giles, Daniel, Governor
Raikes, Tho. Dep. Gov.
Beachcroft, Samuel
Bochim, Roger
Boddingham, Thomas
Boſanquet, Samuel
Champion, Alexander
Coney, Bicknell
Darrell, Edward
Dorrien, George
Harman, Jeremiah
Lewis, Thomas
Long, Beeſton

Mathew, Job
Melluiſh, William
Neave, Sir Richard
Nutt, Joſeph
Oſborn, Iſaac
Peters, George
Simon, Edward
Thelluſſon, Peter Iſaac
Thornton, Godfrey
Thornton, Samuel
Weyland, Mark
Whitmore, John
Winthorp, Benjamin

26 Bank Direɛtors.—24 Eaſt-India Direɛtors.

BANKERS IN LONDON.

Anderſon, John and Alexander, 17 Philpot-lane
Ayton, Braſſey, Lee, and Strathwaite, 71 Lombard-ſtreet
Braſſey and Tritton, 56 Lombard-ſtreet
Barnett, Hoare, Hill, and Barnett, 62 Lombard-ſtr.
Biddulph, Cox, and Ridge, 43 Charing-Croſs
Birch, Chambers, and Hobbs, 152 New Bond-ſtreet
Bond, John and Son, 2 Exchange-Alley

F   Boldero,

Boldero, Addington, Lushington, and Boldero, 30 Cornhill
Botham, Peter, 8 Old-Jewry
Castle, Powell, Summers, and Wilson, 66 Lombard-street
Child and Co. 1 Fleet-street
Couch, Thomas and Co. 59 Strand
Cox, Merle, and Co. 2 Cox's-court, Little-Britain
Croft, Devaynes, Dawes, and Noble, 39 Pall-Mall
Dennis, Snow, Senbys, and Co. 217 Strand
Devesnie, Cuthbert, Marsh, Creed, and Co. 61 Berner-street
Dimsdales and Barnards, 50 Cornhill
Dorrington, Mellow, Martin, and Harrison, 22 Finch-lane
Dorset, Johnson, Wilkinson, and Berners, 68 Bond-street
Down, Thornton, Free, and Cornwall, 1 Bartholomew-lane
Drummonds and Co. 49 Charing-Cross
Edwards, Smith, and Templar,
Esdaile, Wright, Hammet, and Co. 21, Lombard-str.
Foster, Lubbec, Bosanquet, and Co. 11 Manchester-street
Fullers and Chaltree, 24 Lombard-street
Fullers and Vaughan, 84 Cornhill
Glover, Edwards, Crofs, and Benbow, 79 Lombard-street***
Glynn, Mills, and Mitton, 12 Birchin-lane
Goslings and Sharp, 19 Fleet-street
Hankeys, Chaplin, and Hall, 7 Fenchurch-street
Harcourt, Blake, Sansom, Coastalwaite, and Tanner, 65 Lombard-street
Harley, Cameron, and Son, George-street; Msiauon-house.
Herries, Sir Robert and Co. 16 St. James's-street
Hoares, Fleet-street
Jones, Daniel; Baker, Lloyd, and Co. 43 Lothbury
Ladbrook,

[67]

Ladbroke, Rawlinson, Ladbroke, Parker, and Watson, Bank-Buildings
Langston, Towgood, and Amory, 29 Clement's-lane
Lefevre, Currie, Yellowley, and Raikes, 29 Cornhill
Lockharts, Maxton, Wallis, and Clark, 34 Pall-Mall
Martin, Stone, and Foot, 68 Lombard-street
Masters, Dawson, Brooks, Kirton, and Dixon, Chancery-lane
Middleton, Johnson, and Wedgwood, 18 Stratford-place
Masterman, Peters, Walker, and Middleton, 2 White-Hart-court, Gracechurch-street
Maddox, Hodsell, and Michael, near Catherine-street, Strand
Moffat, Kennington, and Styer, 20 Lombard-street
Newman, Anderson, and Lynn, 83 Cornhill
Newman, Havert, Drummond, and Tibbets, 9 Mansion-House-street
Nightingales, 70 Lombard-street***
Ransom, Morland, and Hammersley, 57, Pall-Mall
Roberts, Curtis, Ware, Hornihold, Berwick, and Co. 35 Cornhill
Saunders, Harrison, Pricket, and Newman, Mansion-House-street
Prescott, Grote, Colverden, and Hollingsworth, Threadneedle-street
Pybus, Cole, Grant, and Holl, 148 Old-Bond-street
Sykes, Smith, and Smyth, Mansion-House-street
Smyth, Paine, and Smyth, George-street, Mansion-House
Smyth and Co. 6, Old-Broad-street
Smith, Son, and Co. 73 Lombard-street
Staples and Co. 79 Cornhill***
Stephenson, Batson, Remmington, and Smith, 69 Lombard-street
Taylor, Lloyd, Bowman, Hanber, and Co. 60 Lombard-street
Wilpole, Walpole, Clark, and Sisson, 28, Lombard-st

Walwyn,

Walwyn, Petrie, Ward, and George, 150 New-Bond-ſtreet
Welch, Rogers, Holding, and Rogers, 3 Freeman's-court, Cornhill
Whiteheads, 5 Baſinghall-ſtreet
Wilkinſon, Wilks, Dickinſon, Goodall, and Fiſher, 33 Poultry
Wilkinſon, Polhill, Bloxham, Pinhorn, and Bullock, Southwark
Williams, Son, and Drury, 20 Birchin-lane
Wells, Wood, Percival, and Clark, 76 Lombard-ſtr.
Wright, Selby, and Robinſon, 5 Henrietta-ſtreet, Covent-Garden
Vere, Luccadore, Troughton, Luccado, and Smart, 77 Lombard-ſtreet

It appears from the foregoing liſt of Bank-Directors, India Directors, private bankers in town and country, penſioners, and ſtock-jobbers, that not leſs than three thouſand families are ſupported in every luxury, at the ſame time amaſſing the moſt enormous fortunes, on the ſpoils of the induſtrious part of the community; and their only utility is in ſhuffling paper from hand to hand! It is a moſt extraordinary circumſtance to be conſidered, what can have become of the enormous profits obtained by the Bank of England; as no man that inveſtigates the ſubject can ſay it is leſs than 40 per cent. per annum, and which is proved in page 42 of this pamphlet. What then becomes of the ſurplus—where is the vortex—in what channel does it run—where does it empty itſelf, and where are the locuſts that ſwallow it? Who can tell ſo well as the Bank Directors?

The conſequences of Eaſt-India merchandize being monopolized by a Company, are the commutation tax and an additional window-tax. The duties on tea were lowered, as a compenſation for the above tax, which enabled the Company to lower the price to the conſumer; but tea being an article ſo much in con-ſumption, fumption, they foon faw what effect their powers of monopoly muft have on the neceffitous public, and have brought it nearly to its original price; fo that the additional duties on windows, inftead of fupporting the ftate, is fwallowed up by this monopolizing Company. That neceffary food rice, being an entire and an excellent fubftitute for bread in the Eaft-Indies, and fold there at the moderate price of 6s. per hundred weight, or ¾ per pound, and in England at the Company's fales at 23s. per hundred weight or 2½d. per pound, is another proof that none of the neceffaries can be obtained on reafonable terms, when monopolized by an opulent Company. Among our new conquefts we are boafting of the great additions to our fpice-iflands; but inftead of the price of fpices being lower, a nutmeg that ufed to be fold for three halfpence, now fells for fixpence.

There are fixty-nine private banking houfes in London, three of which are become bankrupts within thefe two laft years, (equal to thirty failures in twenty years) which muft diftrefs and deprive many refpectable families of their property; a circumftance that cannot happen, provided the new fyftem of finance takes place. It appears that the profits of banking are fo exravagant, that the principals take no active part in the bufinefs, and have nothing more to do than ftudy luxuries to fpend their profits on. That this kind of conduct tends to increafe the prices of the neceffaries of life is too obvious for me to enter into particulars, but it is a fact that there are at leaft three thoufand families rolling in gilded carriages drawn by high-fed horfes, whofe provifions, or the produce of the fame land, would fupport great numbers of the induftrious poor that are now wanting the neceffaries of life. This mifchief is fupported by what Mr. Pitt calls the immenfe property of the country, paper circulating medium, which was fcarcely known here, till within the prefent century. It commenced with the

the Bank of England, and from thence it remained a long time in its infancy; for in the year 1743 bankers were of so little confequence, that they were not even mentioned in the court calendar for that year. It is fince that period that we have had fo much reafon to complain of the intolerable increafe of the price of every neceffary of life; for without the extravagant increafe of paper circulating medium, fo much boafted of by Mr. Pitt, the merchants would not have ability to monopolize.

A General View of the Progrefs of the Public Revenue fince the Conqueft. By Sir John Sinclair.

William the Conqueror	£.400,000
William Rufus	350,000
Henry I.	300,000
Stephen	250,000
Henry II.	200,000
Richard I.	150,000
John	100,000
Henry III.	80,000
Edward I.	150,000
Edward II.	100,000
Edward III.	154,140
Richard II.	130,000
Henry IV.	100,000
Henry V.	76,643
Henry VI.	64,976
Edward IV. ⎫ Edward V. ⎬ Richard III. ⎭	100,000
Henry VII.	400,000
Henry VIII.	800,000
Edward VI.	400,000
Mary	450,000
Elizabeth	500,000

James

		£
James I.	— —	600,000
Charles I.	— —	895,000
Commonwealth	— —	1,517,247
Charles II.	— —	1,800,000
James II.	— —	2,001,855
William III.	— —	3,895,205
Anne, at the Union	— —	5,691,803
George I.	⎫	6,762,643
George II.	⎬ including Scotland	8,522,549
George III.	⎭	15,572,974

Statement of the Sums laid out on Great Britain and Ireland.

	£
Nett produce of the revenue —	17,000,000
Charges of management and collection	1,379,822
Counties and allowances —	536,180
Poor rates and county expences	2,100,588
Charitable donations —	258,710
Public Hospitals, including Greenwich	250,000
Turnpikes in Great Britain —	500,000
Parochial assessments and statute labour	100,000
Income of English incorporate towns	500,000
Ditto of Scottish —	100,000
Navigable rivers, canals, &c. —	150,000
Lighting, watching, and paving the streets	200,000
Civil establishment in Scotland —	100,000
Income and taxes of Ireland	2,030,000
Income of the clergy & lay impropriations	5,000,000
	30,175,300
Additional annual interest on the next peace	6,000,000
Considerable addition in army expences	
Management charged by the Bank of England, for payment of dividends, &c.	300,000
	36,475,300

A General

[72]

A General View of the Number of Inhabitants and Public Revenues of the Principal States in Europe.

	Number of Inhabitants.	Revenue. £.
Turkey	18,000,000	5,000,000
Russia	24,000,000	5,800,000
Prussia	(I can't learn)	3,600,000
Sweden	3,300,000	1,000,000
Denmark & Norway	2,300,000	1,000,000
Holland	3,200,000	4,000,000
Austria & Netherlands	21,500,000	12,400,000
Emperor. German dominions		
Hanover		900,000
Saxony		1,100,000
Bavaria and Palatinate		1,100,000
France, before Revolution	26,000,000	18,000,000
Spain	7,400,000	5,000,000
Portugal	6,000,000	1,800,000
Sardinia	—	1,100,000
Sicily	—	1,400,000
Venice	—	1,000,000
		66,200,000
Great Britain		36,425,300

Papal Revenue.	Roman Crowns.
From the clergy	£.100,000
Peter's pence	100,000
Subsidies	100,000
Ship money and customs	400,000
Horse tax	300,000
Post	6,000
Public pledge office	52,000
Chancery, &c.	600,000
Quadering de carn	160,000
Lights of Talfa	185,000
Bologna	720,000
Spoletto	10,000
Various others	1,717,000
	4,500,000

Simon Pope's Letter to Curtis, late Lord Mayor of London.

The whole of this letter is replete with flattery, want of information, want of sincerity and truth. Mr. Pope arrogates to this country the title of the emporium of the world, without a single proof of his knowing the situation of any other kingdom or state. If we are the richest, how is it that we find such immense wealth in Dutch and Spanish ships, when taken as prizes? And to what an astonishing increase is the trade of America, on account of their being so lightly loaded with taxes! Mr. Pope is most wonderfully liberal in his plaudits of his Lordship's generosity in entertainments, exceeding all others in public magnificence; he says his Lordship has been instrumental in lowering the price of bread; but he does not tell us, whether the extravagant expence was paid by his Lordship, or from the overflowing treasury of the corporation; who are now considering the most frugal means of borrowing 100,000l. to lend to Government; nor does he tell us in what way he has been instrumental in lowering the price of bread. Does he wish to refer us to his monopoly? Or can he prove that he was bountiful in rewarding the night-workers employed in emptying damaged corn into the Thames, occasioned by monopoly? Or can he prove that his Lordship ever sold three halfpenny cakes for a penny? His plaudits of the Minister are easily accounted for. An additional 200,000,000l. to the funded debt brings a pretty parcel of half crowns amongst the storks. This Mr. Simon finds to be a ready penny, though the principal be never paid. He charges Mr. Paine with a miserable detail of Dr. Price's errors; but how does he account for the heaven-born Minister's making use of the very worst of them? People that complain of a debt of 500,000,000l. he compares to croaking vermin; but, Simon may depend on it, the

eyes

eyes of the people are opening, and the day is not far diſtant, that, when your ſtock-brokers and ſtock-jobbers will look as much like toads upon pitch-forks as the preſent oppreſſed multitude that he now treats with ſo much contempt. He ſays, the ſupplies are amply provided for; but he does not tell us the proviſion is paper. He tells us of the licentiouſneſs of the preſs, becauſe we complain of this ſwindling iniquity, which draws from the profits of the people's labour 15,000,000l. annually in hard caſh to ſupport the table of Faro. This, with a peace eſtabliſhment, is a ſum equal to three farthings in the penny of the amount of all the profits of their labour, on which Simon and the ſtock jobbing ſwindlers riot in every luxury; and, no doubt, like the liberal fat rector from the pulpit, recommend to the hands of induſtry bread, water, ſtraw, and contentment, though neither bread nor ſtraw are eaſily obtained. He inſults the public, by ſaying that the reſources are more productive than the expenditure. He ſays, if there was any deficiency, individuals would ſoon ſee. Individuals have ſeen, and do now ſee. Witneſs the late Dr. Price, Mr. Paine, and myſelf, with many others. But where is the uſe of foreſight, when the hands of fraudulent chicanery are ſo numerous and powerful? But I hope and believe this race of iniquity is nearly run down.

Why did the French inſolvency take place, which Simon treats with ſo much contempt, but becauſe the multitude, during their abſolute monarchy, would not ſuffer themſelves to be ſwindled out of the profits of their labour by ſtock-jobbers? At the preſent time, I am told, they have inflicted the puniſhment of death, at leaſt paſſed a law, that the gallows is to be the portion of ſtock-jobbers. Simon ſhould conſider a law in England like this may ſoon bring him and ſome of his fraternity to croaking.

In his 12th page he ſays, 'Look into the transfer
' books, and you will find that 19,125,300 l. by an o-
' verflow

'verflow of the revenue, purchafed by a fum of
' 14,350,847 l. 6s. 6d.' How dares he infult the
public with fuch an impudent falfity! Let us look
into the ſtock books, and we ſhall find that at the
rate of 200,000,000l. on the average of 3l. per cent.
have been funded, or muſt be ſo, before Mr. Pitt's
expenditure is provided for: (Mafter Simon ſhould be
told that this is additional.) And if we examine the
price of money bought and ſold by the Miniſter, wo
ſhall find that 7,000,000l. have been waſted of the
public money, in order to carry on the deception of
leſſening the debt. Note, that 45l. 16s. 8d. per cent.
was paid by premium on all the money borrowed and paid
by Mr. Pitt, from Jan. 1786, to Feb. 1794. This is
the effect on the public of political chicanery. Look
at the eſtimate in his pamphlet. And yet he has the
audacity to ſay that Mr. Pitt hath relieved the people
by his care. Wicked Simon! there is not a grain
of modeſty or truth in his aſſertion. He ſays, it is
much to be lamented that the lower orders of the
community have not a capacity to diſcover fallacies
impoſed on their ſenſes. It is to be lamented; and
the only circumſtance that cauſed the ſtock-jobbing
chicanery to have run ſuch an extenſive courſe.
Our intelligent ſtock-broker tells us, that we may
content ourſelves, that a great part of our earnings is
ſpent in luxury and extravagance, and therefore we
may eaſily reconcile the impoſitions. Now every
thinking man muſt know that every deſcription of
waſteful extravagance is an additional cauſe of ſcarc-
ity. If waſteful extravagance was ſufficient to excuſe
the plunderer in high life, why not the thief in low life?
Few of them would find any difficulty in proving their
extravagance, if it would ſave them from the gallows.

He ſays, that every member of the ſtate is bound, in
common juſtice, to contribute proportional to his
ſituation. Does the ſtockjobber or loan-monger, do
thoſe that make their 100,000l. the profit of the day,
who, to the end of his life, from that day's work
, alone,

alone, may roll in his gilded equipage, and feed himself with every luxury, at the expence of the labour of the starving poor? Simon seems to extend his ideas relative to the increased riches of the country, on account of the great profits arising from goods imported from India. He may prove the India Company's importations are immensely great, and their profits are extravagant; but as they are sold to, paid for, and consumed by, the inhabitants of this country, how does it appear that the riches of this country are increased by importations from India? But from this circumstance alone he values the increased riches of the country, to the amount of hundreds of millions. In his 43d page he says, 'The minister brings 'forward his loans, and, whatever their magnitude, 'they are amply provided for.' But how are they provided for? By the loan-monger, with new coinage of paper, (Master Simon should be taught this is no proof of stability) but new mortgages on the labour of the people, as the people must find hard cash to pay the most extravagant and usurious interest.

In the same page he says, there are four hundred and eleven banking-houses, in town and country; that each must have a capital of 100,000l. to carry on their business, without which they could not exist, and he estimates their property to be 41,100ol. But if he wishes to strike a fair balance, the whole of this extravagant increase of property will be found wanting.

Respecting the property of bankers, which you estimate at 41,100,000l. of this estimate you must give up the total, as the whole of the country business in banking is carried on by the bankers notes and their customers cash; and I believe the town business much by the same means. I knew a house in the country that were in the habits of making profits to the amount of sixteen thousand pounds per annum, and their principal clerk acknowledged the proprietors had not a guinea of their own money employed in it these last twenty years—the discounts,

con-

consisting of the cash of their customers, and their own notes, coined for the purpose of discounting. Such circumstances as these are general throughout the kingdom. So that if Mr. Pope can be guided by facts, he must give up the 41,100,000l. that he claims as the riches of the nation, as the property of the bankers.

Thus Mr. Pitt's funding 200,000,000 l. and the unaccountable riches of the merchants, Mr. Pope values at 4,000,000,000l. which, by a just estimate, will be found no more than one fourth part of the sum; as the land-tax of the kingdom, when you average the tax at two shillings in the pound, and at twenty-five years purchase, is worth 500,000,000l. Cash and chattels are not likely to exceed that sum. Therefore one thousand millions must be the extent of the value of this kingdom.

Mr. Pope says that twenty millions annually is pregnant with no alarm, and that it is only one shilling in the pound, on eleven millions six hundred and sixty-five thousand four hundred and forty pounds, paid annual interest. Mr. Pope might as well have charged us with the whole we have to pay, which cannot be now less than fifteen millions annually for interest.

But, Master Pope may be asked, how comes it that the poors' rates are as much complained of, though the annual amount is but a little more than two millions. The payers complain that it amounts to four shillings, some say five, and others as much as six shillings in the pound; and yet Mr. Pope says, that 11,665,440l. is not more than one shilling in the pound. Are stock-jobbers and stock-brokers so much ashamed of the truth, that they will mix none with their writings? I have been told that our heaven-born Minister spoke the truth for once. It has been reported that he should say, he would spend every guinea in the kingdom rather than the war should

should end. In fact it hath been spent more than once.

Simon might have congratulated his Majesty on being the richest prince in Europe, or the world—for I believe he is so. I can account for his being worth twenty millions. In the year 1760 his grandfather left him four millions, which alone must have produced the sum I give him credit for, by compound interest.

In 15 years 4 millions must
  amount to £. 8,000,000
In 15 years 8 millions, compound inter. 16,000,000
  6 years 16 ditto, considerably more
  than ——————— 4,000,000

36 years accumulation, with compound interest on four millions 20,000,000

This statement must be admitted, supposing his Majesty has made no profit by stock-jobbing, and has spent every shilling of the sums annually granted him by Parliament, which is not likely to be the case. Quere, to what amount may we rate his Majesty's present income?

Interest of his fortune, at 5l. per cent. £.1,000,000
Civil list   900,000
Forfeitures, fines, &c.   600,000

Annual income   —   —   2,500,000

nearly equal to 50,000l. per week, equal to 7000 pounds per day. This we may call the richest prince in Europe, or perhaps the world. These are the immense riches of a prince, when hundreds of thousands of his subjects have not more than 3d. per day to live on; so that his Majesty's income is full as much as 560,000 of his poor, half-starved subjects.

In the present little tract I mean to take but little or no more notice of Simon Pope, only, that however it may be out of the habit of stock-jobbers, I
                                                 would

would advife him once more to mix fome facts, if ever he intends another addrefs to the public; which, perhaps, he means to leave until he finds another fuch liberal chief magiftrate as Citizen Curtis.

In the early part of Mr. Pitt's adminiftration I was ready to have joined in the common cry of " Pitt " for ever." But firft I had made up my mind, and determined to be better informed: and I foon found that our young cherubim kept bad company, and fuch as I thought more likely to bring him to the gibbet, than to produce him any fubftantial credit as a ftatefman. One of the perfons alluded to is Charles, firnamed Catchpenny. This Mr. Catchpenny Mr. Pitt was loading with honours, places, and penfions, to an enormous amount, though a halter would have been a more fuitable reward. During Lord North's adminiftration, Mr. Catchpenny was paymafter in this, that, and almoft every lucrative department that was worth notice: the ufual commiffions I am told produced from forty to fifty thoufand pounds annually. But all this would not do for Mr. Catchpenny. In the fhort interim of a change in adminiftration Mr. Catchpenny was called upon to make up his account, and pay the balance. But what was the defence of this fwindle-cap fenator? Two hundred thoufand pounds was on mortgage, and owing to the diftreffed fituation of the landholders, Lord Mansfield would not admit of foreclofures, and therefore he could not pay the balance. Thus had this man drawn from the treafury 200,000l. more than he could ufe in the line of his employment, and made ufe of it, placing it to intereft, as I am told, for his own private emolument, which produced him a profit of 10,000l. per annum. But note, that this fum, in the way it was borrowed, coft the public at leaft 10l. per cent. which created a lofs of 20,000l. per annum. This was one of our heaven-born minifter's favourites, whom he receives with open arms, takes him to St. James's to be inoculated

culated with noble blood—and this lump of corruption, this rotten sheep, he turns into the herd of lordly lambs; of course spreads the infection to such a degree, that the price of mutton, with every other necessary of life, has been extravagantly dear ever since.

Executions opposite the Debtors' Door, Newgate, from December 12, 1792, *to October* 30, 1793.

1793
    Philip Davey and John Bone, for Forgery and
       Felony — — —   2
    John Brown, Wm. Graham, and Thomas Folkes,
       for Felony and Robberies —   3
Feb. 20, Wm. Bateman ⎫
         George Hobbard, alias Lord Massey ⎪
         Thomas Healy ⎪
         Thomas Montague Glover ⎬ 8
         George Ranken ⎪
         Abraham Mayhew ⎪
         Francis Pope ⎪
         Isaac More, for stealing a 10l. Bank-
            note out of a letter ⎭
April 10, James Field — — 1
May 29, Alexander Elder — — 1
         James Banner — — 1
June 26, John Patterson — — 1
                                         ———
         Total number executed   17

Suppose the amount of each of the above felonies had been equal to that of Isaac More, 10l. total 170l. Mr. Catchpenny at the rate of 10,000l. per annum, but I do not know the length of time: a part of it may have continued to this day. Was Mr. Catchpenny hanged? No, no: Mr. Pitt will not consent to the hanging of men that are high in office, nor the calling of them to any account. The proprietor of
                                                    Holwood

Holwood-House might be the next. Mr. Catchpenny enjoys a number of places under Government, and titles in abundance.

It was not my intention to have troubled my readers again with Mr. Pope's complimentary letter to Citizen Curtis, but Mr. Pope says that the profits of the Bank of England are about 300,000l. annually. What could be his motive, I am at a loss to account for, unless the Bank of England were ashamed of their extravagance, and had hired master Pope to bury nine tenths of it, in hopes to conceal it from the eyes of the public. Their profits are four millions annually, nearly forty per cent. on their capital, which has been proved in this work; but Mr. Pope says their pond is always full of cash, for that it runs in as fast as it runs out—but this he cannot possibly prove, unless he proves that the cash returns into the Bank as fast from Prussia, Sardinia, and the Emperor, as it ran out. Mr. Pope is boasting of three hundred millions, as an overflow of riches to this country, and gives credit to Mr. Pitt for the spending two hundred millions, just in the same way as though the nation had acquired so much riches from his wasteful extravagance.

One of the dangers Mr. Pope complains of is that if Mr. Pitt had not run the nation so much in debt, the influx of property must have been laid out in land. Now any man that will investigate must know that no such property is in existence as three hundred millions, nor a twentieth part of that sum; and that the holders of the immense paper circulation have acquired their nominal riches by shuffling paper from hand to hand. As a proof of this assertion, let me refer you to the opulent Corporation of the city of London, who have determined to lend Government one hundred thousand pounds, but whose first object must be how to borrow it on the most frugal terms. The opulent East-India Company are also about to lend Government two millions without interest, on the following liberal conditions;

ditions; viz. 'You muſt allow us to increaſe our capital two millions, by which we ſhall clear a profit (at the preſent low price of 170l. per cent.) of one million four hundred thouſand pounds—in that caſe we will lend you two millions (perhaps of their bonds for ſix months) without intereſt.'

It ſeems that the India-Company have ſold goods unpaid to the amount of   —   £.2,250,000
Value of goods in England unſold   5,629,926
                                           £.7,879,926

But what are the richeſt goods worth in a country where there is no money to buy them? If they were to ſend them to Germany, no doubt but the Emperor or his ſubjects could buy them; and what a comfortable balance it would be in favour of England!

In anſwer to Mr. Pope. The value of land has dropped in England from the circumſtance of there having been little or no money to purchaſe it for theſe laſt thirty years, but no abatement of rental has taken place, ſo as to enable the farmer to have brought his produce to market on better terms, but the very reverſe; though the lands have loſt in their ſales near fifty per cent., ſuch as ſold formerly at thirty years purchaſe, will not now yield more than twenty years purchaſe. Can Simon Pope perſuade any man that Government have imported 450,000 quarters of wheat at 5l. 5s. the quarter, at the expence of 13s. 1½d. the Wincheſter buſhel? or that five hundred ſhips have arrived in England with nine hundred quarters each of foreign wheat, for which he knows Government have paid 2,362,500l. and that this money hath been borrowed at an extravagant intereſt, with a chance of 100l. per cent. premium, which is only ſimilar to what Mr. Pitt hath been paying? Mr. Pope tells us there are innumerable private hoards of caſh in this country; private I ſuppoſe they may be, and ſo much ſo as never to make any public appearance.

                                                       Mr.

Mr. Pope says it would be unjust as well as ungrateful not to bestow the highest commendations on the very judicious and successful efforts of Administration; so that, according to Mr. Pope's account, the highest commendations must arise to Government, equal to the heighth they have been the means of advancing the price of that necessary article for the support of life, wheat, by prohibiting the importation, when it was advanced from 5s. the Winchester bushel to 1l. 6s. 3d. Though the whole of the extravagant price of wheat does not fall immediately on that article, yet such hath been the expence of procuring it, which must be made up on other taxes. This is the effect of our virtuous Administration prohibiting the importation of wheat, unless it bore a higher price than 6s. 8d. the Winchester bushel. Were not the members of this virtuous administration the first importers after the price became exorbitant? and was it not sold for the utmost farthing it would bring in all the markets of the kingdom? What became of the profits must be best known to our virtuous administration.——So much consistency is there in our public writer Mr. Simon Pope, that after toiling over forty-eight pages for the particular purpose of abusing Mr. Paine, he tells Citizen Curtis that ' it would be paying too great a compliment to Mr. Paine to appear angry with him.'

Soame Jenyns says that wheat is as much taxed as though the taxation fell upon the article itself: but Simon Pope says, the wisdom and humanity of Government are to be admired, on account of their having provided against a scarcity of wheat. Now let me explain what hath been the conduct of this virtuous Government. When wheat was at the moderate price of five shillings the Winchester bushel, our virtuous Administration thought it too cheap; and Lord Sheffield and Mr. Pitt said the poor would live too well: though, by the bye, I have known it sold in England for one-half of the money.

It is now but fair to state what effect the prohibition has had on the price of corn. Wheat rose from five shillings the Winchester bushel to an enormous price never before heard of in this country. The virtuous Administration began to think they should want bread themselves; and then, to prove their wisdom and humanity, Mr. Pope says that Government hath sent 2,362,500l. out of the kingdom, to pay for 450,000 quarters of wheat, at the rate of five guineas the quarter of eight Winchester bushels.

Price of the Winchester bushel, at 5l. 5s per quarter, is — — 0 13 1½

The next thing to be remarked is, how the money was obtained for the purchase of this corn. The money was borrowed, and at the rate of 100l. per cent. to the subscriber, even if paper answered the purpose for payment, in the end the price must be double to the consumer — 0 13 1½

─────────

1 6 3

Cost to the consumer, at eight gallons the Winchester bushel, or the quartern loaf, allowance for baking, &c. — 0 1 9

in the stead of 5d. which would have been most probably the case if our virtuous Administration had taken no part in prohibiting the importation of wheat when it was at the moderate price of five shillings the bushel. But if Simon Pope should take it in his head to insult the public a second time, I have no doubt but he will say that through the wisdom of Mr. Pitt the public are indulged with time for payment; but Simon, let it not be thought an indulgence, while the public have near six per cent. annual interest to pay on the sums so advanced for the purchase of wheat.

I do

I do not reflect on Administration for the importation of wheat; but that part of it which was landed at Liverpool and several other ports, was sold at a most extravagant price for their own emolument. —The mayor of Liverpool, in his letter to the virtuous administration, hoped to have the price lowered, but was answered that the broker was to abide by his orders in the sale, which I think was fifteen shillings the Winchester bushel—another instance of the humanity of our virtuous administration! Mr. Pitt says that charity begins at Holwood-House. I am told that the heavenly minister having three or four of his guardian angels about him, viz. Charles Catchpenny, Harry India-House, and a brother secretary, prior to the last additional duty on wine taking place, candidly opened his mind to them respecting the tax; they all wisely took the hint, and, notwithstanding their extravagant emoluments, they and a few friends who were in the secret, can for seven years to come, get drunk 25 per cent. cheaper than any other men in the kingdom.

The Contrast. Poor Humphry Bowering, who lived at Cullumpton, in Devonshire, from his birth to the age of about sixty years, and I believe was charged with no other crime than honest poverty, died for the want of the common necessaries of life; whose habitation was within one hundred yards of that of Robert Baker, worth a hundred thousand pounds, (I mistake, he was only in the possession of a hundred thousand pounds, though in fact worth nothing.)—Cullumpton is a place very badly situated for fuel, so that the poor inhabitants can purchase nothing but wood, which is sold to them by this Cullumpton Dives, the wood-land in the neighbourhood being chiefly his own property, lest his poor neighbourhood should get too great a bargain for their penny. I have no reason to doubt the fact as to poor Humphry Bowering. When I was in that town about three years since, I called to see an old friend, where I met a poor man who told me that he was in the habit of doing errands for that family, which kept him from starving, as the parish would allow him no more than sixpence per week. Cullumpton has a numerous poor and the payers in general are not rich. If this was the case in the country, what a number of inhabitants might there not have been in the metropolis lying on bare boards with craving appetites, whilst the Lord-Mayor was rolling in his gilded chariot towards his brilliant illuminated mansion, to meet his august and Right Honourable friends, loaded with every luxury, at the expence of five thousand pounds for the night's entertainment—which sum amounts to one shilling in the pound of the profit of one day's stock-jobbing. The expence of the night is said to have been five thousand pounds, exclusive of the following charges. (See the Address to the Freemen of London, here introduced.) This could not be the case when the Lord Mayor's expences were limited to twenty pounds. It was then that the cottager enjoyed the use of his own brass kettle, his bushel of malt for 2s. and a fine leg of mutton for 1s. 6d. but this cannot be the case again till stock-jobbing makes its exit, or while a hundred thousand pounds profit is made by a Lord-Mayor or by a Thelusson on the profit of a single loan!—this can only be prevented by an entire new system of finance.

The following are copies of two letters on the iniquity of private tontines, addressed to the Editor of the Corresponding Society's Magazine, and which were inserted in the Numbers of that work for June and July 1796:—

Perceiving the disadvantage under which the public gamed in these tontines, it was my design to expose the case by suitable calculations, but other employments intervened. The managers of one of these schemes

W
be carri
the Mi
juſt and
Corporat
Buſineſs.
(as repor
during t
is preſent
Mr. Dan
£.25 o

25 13

No doubt an
price of labour
(in his Wealth c
of which I infer

Years.	Price o quarte wheat year.	
	L.	S.
1202 to 1204	0	12
1205	0	13
	0	15
1237	0	3
1243	0	2
1244	0	2
1246	0	16
1287	0	3

advance muft have taken place in the
fince the period at which Dr. Smith
f Nations) ftates the price of wheat;
a few abftracts.

the [...] each	Bufhel, of 9 gallons		Price of the quartern of flour, or loaf, exclufive of the expence of baking
D.	S.	D.	
0	1	6	1 penny half-farthing
4	1	8	1 penny half-farthing
0	1	10½	1 penny half-farthing
4	0	5	1 farthing
0	0	3	half-farthing
0	0	3	half-farthing
0	2	0	3 pence
4	0	5	1 farthing
8	0	1	half-farthing
0	0	1½	half-farthing

schemes having however, divided their capital, at the expiration of seven years and a half, I have nothing to do now, but to state the facts relative to that scheme, in order to shew how greatly the subscribers were wronged by it.

Each subscriber paid 6s. 6d. per quarter, together with 6d. per quarter to the managers for their trouble, which together, in seven years (the term for which the tontine was established) amounted to 9l. 16s.

Each of the surviving subscribers received, on the division of the capital, 10l. 2s. So that 6s. only was received by each subscriber for the interest of his money, and the benefit arising from survivorship.

Let us now endeavour to calculate the sum drawn from the public by the projectors of these schemes, for the trouble of management. I knew of six of these plans; two in London, two in Bristol, and two in Yorkshire. There might be more, but the evil will appear sufficiently extensive if there were not. The agent of one of the societies in Bristol boasted, by public advertisement, that its subscribers amounted to more than 120,000; but taking the average of the six societies to be 80,000 each, the whole of the subscribers to these plans would be 480,000 persons. These paid each 2s. per annum for management, which in seven years would produce 336,000l. But to this sum must be added six months interest of the whole capital produced by the subscriptions; because the managers did not divide till six months after the expiration of the term, on the pretence of settling their books. The produce of 480,000 subscriptions, at 9l. 16s. each, is 4,704,000l. the half year's interest on which, at 5 per cent. is 117,600l. making, with the money received by the projectors for the article of management, the enormous sum of 453,600l.

I need not dwell on this statement. It is accurate; and no words can add to its eloquence. I shall be happy if this paper save a portion of your numerous readers,

readers, who may be tempted to subscribe to some of these schemes, from being a prey to their delusive promises.

June 14th, 1796.   Thomas Fry.

Citizen Editor,   July 20, 1796.

When I wrote my former letter to you on the subject of private tontines, I thought that a statement of the probable amount of the sums *divided by the managers*, would be sufficient to save your readers from *the imposition of that species of taxation*. But the schemes in question are addressed so powerfully to the passion of cupidity, that I think it right to expose other parts of this evil; and I hope you will spare me, for this purpose, a page or two of your magazine for this month.

I have stated the sum received on the whole subscriptions for management at 453,600l. But this is not the whole of the money (enormous as it is) of which the industrious are plundered in this way. I have made calculations, grounded on the bills of mortality) of the probable profit of survivorship, including compound interest, to each subscriber, and I find it to be 2l. 17s. 2d. Your limits will not permit me to expect that you should state these calculations. They are made with candour, and, I believe, with as much accuracy as the subject will admit of; nevertheless, I invite any person who thinks I misapprehend the matter, to make calculations for himself, and meanwhile I proceed on my calculations as data in the case.

The amount of the benefit of survivorship, on the whole subscriptions, I calculate (on the same data) to be 980,408l. 6s. 8d. Let us see how much of this is accounted for by the managers. They received 453,600l. for management, and they paid 6s. to each of the surviving subscribers; that is to say, they paid 102,900l. to the whole of the surviving subscribers, reckoning the number to be 343,000, which I take to be a fair average; and these sums together make 556,500l. Let this

this be deducted from 980,408l. 6s. 8d. (the produce of furvivorſhip, as above ſtated) and there will remain 423,908l. 6s. 8d. unaccounted for by the managers.

What became of this ſum? Was it ſunk by the difference in the price of the funds at the reſpective times of buying in, and the time of ſelling out, in order to divide the capital? Perhaps that was the caſe, as the funds fell greatly during that period. But my complaint is, that enormous ſums of money are transferred from the pockets of the ſubſcribers into thoſe of men who give no equivalent for thoſe ſums; no leſs than the ſum of 453,600l. to the managers, in every caſe, whatever is to become of the ſubſcriber's profit (which we have ſeen was 6s. for ſeven years and a half on 9s. 16s.) and 423,908l. 6s. 8d. loſt by the mode of managing the buſineſs, although one of the lures thrown out to the public has been a promiſe of great profit from the management, by buying into the funds, over and above the profit of ſurvivorſhip, and of compound intereſt.

But this is not all: there ſtill remains another point to be cleared up. The ſubſcribers are amuſed with an opinion of poſſeſſing ſecurities for their capital, which they have not. They are told of ſums being inveſted from time to time in the Bank, in the names of reſpectable perſons, and they believe *thoſe perſons* are ſecurity to them. Whereas they have no ſecurity *but the projectors and managers of the reſpective plans*. It is true, the managers are not likely to become defaulters, while they draw ſuch a *prodigious revenue* from their ſchemes; for that would be to kill the gooſe for her eggs. But if the management of any of theſe tontines ſhould fall into the hands of deſperate men, who ſhould loſe the whole, or the greater part of the capital in ſpeculations, there would be no remedy for the ſubſcribers; and in theſe times of very general deſperation, there is no great ſecurity that this may not happen.

THOMAS FRY.

In the new-fangled scheme for the present lottery, a circumstance of deception is practised that never entered the brain of any other person but our heaven-born minister, by which the adventurers are deprived of one hundred thousand pounds on the value of their prizes. It is said in the bill, that 60,000 tickets amount to 500,000l. The usual and fair mode used to be to mention the intrinsic value of each, (usually 10l. but now reduced to 8l. 6s. 8d.) and the following ought to have been the statement: 60,000 tickets at 8l. 6s. 8d. each, amount to 500,000l. so that the most illiterate adventurer would have been informed what he had to game for.

I have now by me bills of mortality and calculations for the benefit of age, which will prove the following trifling subscriptions equal to its support; and by which mankind in the lowest situations in life, at a trifling expence, may secure an independence when they become aged. But the limits of this little tract, on account of a variety of new matter, will not admit of it, nor is there any necessity or even utility in bringing it forward, while Mr. Pitt's solid securities (as he calls them) are in existence. The different funded systems that for the present form the rotten foundation, require two for one for its support.

Terms to Subscribers for the benefit of Age.

Every parent or other friend subscribing for an infant under two years of age, the sum of eight shillings annually, or 2s. per quarter, (about a farthing per day) such person will be entitled after they have attained the age of fifty years, to the sum of thirteen pounds annually, or five shillings per week, during their natural life.

Age	Yearly	Quarterly	Yearly	Weekly
2 to 5	10s. or	2s. 6d.	13l.	or 5s.
5 to 10	15s. or	3s. 9d.	13l.	or 5s.
10 to 20	1l. 5s. or	6s. 9d.	13l.	or 5s.
20 to 30	2l. 10s. or	12s. 6d.	11l. 10s.	or 4s. 6d.
30 to 50	3l. 10s. or	17s. 6d.	10l. 8s.	or 4s.

Note, that the annual or quarterly payments muſt increaſe after two years, in the following manner:—third year, 2s. 2d. quarterly; fourth, 2s. 4d. fifth, 2s. 6d. and every claſs muſt add the trifling increaſe, in proportion to the ſums advanced; but no higher premium will be required than 17s. 6d. quarterly, and from thoſe only who neglect ſubſcribing till they arrive at thirty-ſix years of age.

As a proof of the ſtability of the foregoing plan, I will ſtate what capital each ſubſcriber will have in the fund to ſupport his annuity, from compound intereſt and benefit of ſurvivorſhip:

			L.	S.	D.
An infant ſubſcriber under two years of age, paying 2s. quarterly, will at the time he arrives at the age of fifty, have a capital of			186	0	8
5 years	paying	2s. 6d. quarterly	169	17	6
10		3s. 9d.	179	4	3
20		6s. 9d.	152	14	0
30		12s. 6d.	134	6	7
36		17s. 6d.	101	0	10

It is impoſſible to enumerate the vaſt variety of advantages of this plan, but it is ſufficient to ſay for the preſent, that it is proper for clergymen with ſmall livings, officers in the navy, army, exciſe, cuſtoms, &c. with a multitude of the loweſt orders of ſociety, and the pariſh poor would be greatly relieved.

Terms of Mr. Pitt's laſt curious loan for eighteen millions; payment by inſtalments; intereſt to commence 13th of October 1796.

1ſt payment	13th January 1797	10l. per cent.
2d	17th March	10l.
3d	21ſt April	10l.
4th	2d June	10l.
5th	21ſt July	15l.
6th	25th Auguſt	15l.
7th	28th September	15l.
8th	31ſt October	15l.

Bonus

	L.	S.	D.
Bonus — —	12	10	0
Prompt - - -	3	0	0
Interest from 13th October to 13th January, at 6 per cent. —	1	10	0
Ditto from 13th Jan. to 17th Mar. 2 months 4 days on 90l. at 6 per cent.	1	0	0
Ditto from 17th Mar. to 21st April, 1 month 4 days on 80l. at 6 per cent.	0	9	0
Ditto from 21st April to 2d June, 1 month 11 days on 70l. at 6 per cent.	0	9	5
Ditto from 2d June to 21st July, 1 month 19 days on 60l. at 6 per cent.	0	10	0
Ditto from 21st July to 25th August 1 month 4 days on 45l. at 6 per cent.	0	5	1
Ditto from 25th August to 28th September, 1 month 3 days on 30l. at 6 per cent.	0	3	4
Ditto from 28th September to 31st October, 1 month 3 days on 15l. at 6 per cent.	0	1	8
	19	18	6
Expence of buying up, or Commission for Repayment by the Bank of England	0	2	6
Amount of Bonus —	20	1	0
Money subscribed —	100	0	0
	£.120	1	0

If 100l. in the 5 per cents. be worth 120l. what will be the cost of 100l. in the 3 per cents.?—Answer 50l. So that Mr. Pitt is now borrowing paper, in the proportion of 3 per cent. receiving at the rate of 50l. for every hundred; so that this last loan of eighteen millions to have been borrowed in the 3 per cents. at the same rate of interest, 6l. 1s. would have created a new debt to the amount of 36,009,000l. or for every 100l. a new debt of 200l. 16s. 8d.

The

The circumstance of Mr. Fox declaring to God that he had no money to subscribe to this lucrative loan, is ominous to me; for Mr. Fox certainly could not be so ignorant as not to know that loans of Mr. Pitt's could not be filled up without money: nor are we to suppose that Mr. Fox wanted zeal for supporting the credit of his country in so just and necessary a war, for which he hath been so often and so ready in voting the supplies. I cannot conjecture but that Mr. Fox declined from a principle of liberality, as I am told that a number of the lower orders of the clerks to the Bank were dropping in with their ten thousands to fill up—Mr. Fox declined, because he would not deprive a set of men of the bonus, that might want it more than himself.

From the estimates of funding in the Emperor's loan, which must be a money transaction, the annuities converted into three per cents. it appears that Mr. Pitt gives a hundred pounds security to receive 4l. 10s. 8d. But it appears, however, from the last loan of eighteen millions, that paper is to be had on somewhat better terms; for he gets very near 50l. for 100l. securities in the three per cents. As Mr. Pitt hath been in the habit of paying 96l. in the three per cents. it appears that the subscribers are now in the receipt of 6l. 10s. per cent. for money lent in the name of the Emperor, with the prospect of 230l. for every 100l. advanced; and for the loan of paper 6l. 1s. per cent. and for every 100l. advanced the prospect of 190l. And the prospect to be sure must be very great, as Mr. Pitt rates them amongst the solid securities. Mr. Pitt hath certainly undertaken more than he can perform, as steward for the whole kingdom. It is only monied men, paper men, placemen, pensioners, stock jobbers, and stock brokers: but he has thought nothing of the Swinish Multitude.

Simon

Simon Pope declares, that we are the emporium of the world for riches:—surely Simon muſt mean for valuable paper. Paper, in England, will buy ten thouſand ſheep, as many fat oxen, a coach and ſix for my Lord Swindle-cap. But under theſe circumſtances it is impoſſible the lower orders of the people can exiſt, without the privilege of coining paper: therefore, in order to help out the Swiniſh Multitude, I propoſe myſelf as a partner with our heaven-born miniſter, though I do not know that it will be a pleaſing connection. I muſt have the indulgence of coining paper for the uſe of my herd: I do not mean bills of magnitude, but ſuch as will buy quartern loaves, legs of mutton, turnips, &c. with every other neceſſary of life. And when this paper coinage comes into general circulation, we ſhall find that Criſpin Heeltap's note in favour of Mother Wapping will be as good as the Bank of England's. Now as I only wiſh to continue my paper coinage as long as the exigencies of the ſtate are provided for with Bank of England paper, I think my partner cannot refuſe me; for if, during our preſent wants, between rage and deſpair, the devil ſhould enter into my head, and I ſhould take my herd up to a high clift, and we ſhold run into the ſea and be drowned, what is to become of your titled lordlings, placemen, penſioners, ſtock jobbers, &c. you would ſoon get dirty, ragged, and, Egyptian like, have lice in all your borders.

Our burthens have increaſed during the reign of the beſt of kings. In the year 1760 the whole of our funded debt amounted to no more than 75,237,926l. 14s. 2¾d. bearing an annual intereſt of 2,419,313l. 17s. 10½d.

Preſent

Prefent amount of the funded debt, when the outftanding debts are funded and converted into the 3 per cents. —	500,000,000	0 0
Principal debt, 1760 –	75,237,926	14 2
Additional principal debt, in the proportion of 3 per cent.	424,762,073	5 10
Annual intereft of debt, 1794	15,000,000	
Charges of management by the Bank of England —	300,000	
	15,300,000	
Annual intereft of debt, 1760	2,419,313	17 10
Additional annual intereft and management —	12,880,686	2 2

As this change hath taken place in the reign of the beft of kings, we certainly muft have had corrupt Parliaments. As they have acknowledged it themfelves, it can be no treafon to tell them fo. Upon the whole, it is aftonifhing that in the little diftance from St. Stephen's Chapel to the Houfe of Commons, honourable gentlemen fhould in fo fhort a time empty their mouths of their prayers, and immediately fill their hearts with corruption: the ground ought to be confecrated every foot of the way from the chapel to the honourable houfe, which may in future have the wonderful effect of keeping them virtuous. I fhall fay nothing more of the prefent members than pray that God may make them more virtuous, and Simon Pope a better man than his father.

PEACE

PEACE.

But there seemed to be no peace intended. It is my opinion, that if Lord Malmsbury had gone to the French Convention with something like the following proposition, it would be nearer at hand than it seems to be at present.

To the President of the French Convention.

I am come from the King of England with overtures of peace and good will between the two nations. We want not to hold a foot of your territory, nor will we give up any of our own: we wish for mutual friendship, a general intercourse of trade, merchandize on both sides to be unincumbered with taxes, and of course mutual advantages.

Answer of the Convention.

All hail, Citizen Malmsbury! Welcome, Peace!

There certainly cannot be a more honourable peace, or likely to be more lasting, than when one nation does not attempt to take the advantage of another. But before terms like these can be expected to be proposed, we must get rid of our present ministers, loan mongers, and stock jobbers, or no terms will be likely to be produced that will be mutually advantageous, manly, or open.

Mr. Pitt's conduct in retrieving the distresses of the nation hath operated like that of an involved spendthrift attempting to redeem his paternal estate by adding another harlot to his seraglio.

It is extraordinary, but a fact, that most nations in Europe seem to be better acquainted with the true characters of our heaven-born minister and his connections than their own countrymen. We seem to have no sincere alliance but the Emperor, who keeps snug to the English guinea; but we shall find soon
that

that the dearest friends must part. The Duke of Bedford approves of sending another 500,000l. to the Emperor, as it may shew our strength. His Grace puts me in mind of an hiſtorical account of the city of Exeter, which, after a long and tedious ſiege by the Danes, was reduced to half a ſheep in their garriſon, which they politically threw over the wall to their beſieging enemy, and the men wrapping themſelves up in their ſheep-ſkins, crept round the ramparts; this had the deſired effect—the enemy were deceived, and the ſiege broke up. But his Grace ſhould conſider the French have a better knowledge of the ſtrength of our finances than the Danes had of the proviſions in the caſtle of Exeter; they know we are paying nearly 100l. per cent. for the loan of paper as well as we do ourſelves.

Reply of the honeſt Turk to our ambaſſador at Conſtantinople, when Mr. Pitt offered to aſſiſt them in chaſtizing the late Empreſs of Ruſſia:— 'Your vizier or miniſter muſt have ſome project of deception in view, ſome oppreſſive ſcheme, to amuſe your nation, who, we are told, are credulous, ſervile, and adorers of money. Avarice, if we are well informed, is your characteriſtic; you will ſell and buy your God; money is your deity, and all things is commerce with your miniſtry; it has been your practice to embroil all mankind, and thereby profit by your perfidy.' Have we not embroiled other nations, and do we not to this day ſupport the bone of contention, by ſupplying the crowned heads of other nations with caſh, while the people of this country are drained of their laſt guinea, to provide for the intereſt of uſurious contracts, and for which foreign princes barter the blood of their ſubjects. I ſhould not wonder, if at a future day the Emperor ſhould offer to pay us in human carcaſes, as he knows the Elector of Hanover makes thirty pounds a head of his ſubjects.

H FRENCH

FRENCH CODE OF LAWS, February 1792.

The committee of legiflation reported on the mode of enforcing refponfibility of minifters, and of proceeding againft them when accufed of mifconduct; the purport of which was for neglect of duty, or actual violation of the conftitution, they were to be punifhed with death; or for incapacity, or error of judgment, with the lofs of their places; and that both thefe cafes were provided for by the fpirit of the conftitution and the penal code. If there is any fpirit left in the Britifh conftitution, or it was ever neceffary to hang a Britifh minifter, what muft become of our prefent heaven-born minifter?

MONIED MEN,

Their rife, progrefs, and prefent fituation.

It is about one hundred years fince thefe locufts, thefe Bels and Dragons of our age, commenced their operations; which, for the firft fifty years, made very little progrefs. Indeed, it is the laft thirty-five years, in the reign of 'the beft of kings,' that the practice of fwindling hath operated fo much, to the deftruction of the honeft and induftrious part of the community; and during the laft three years, in the reign of William Pitt, the grievance has operated to an equal amount of what was done in threefcore years before him—and yet the eyes of the people are not quite open! To give credit for an original capital employed for the public fervice would be too liberal, fay 10,000,000, and thofe monied men are now in the poffeffion of 500,000,000, without any confiderable additional riches to the country. Indeed, the land of the kingdom that forty years back was worth thirty years purchafe, is not now worth more than twenty years purchafe; of courfe not worth the former price, by at leaft one hundred and fifty millions! and yet we abound in riches—monied men adding to their property by the cart-load.

But how comes all this to bear? The money has been all lent thefe fifty years, and this immenfe nominal property

property has been acquired by shuffling paper from hand to hand, by the first-rate national swindlers. The minister having on every new loan added a new mortgage on the profits of the labours of the people, in order to pay the interest of these iniquitous contracts, without any additional riches to the country. Can we be possessed of so much stupidity as to suppose that because Mr. Pitt hath run the nation two hundred millions in debt, that the nation is two hundred millions the richer for it? It is much the poorer, from his having sent ten millions of specie out of the kingdom, more than one half of its real strength. Simon Pope tells citizen Curtis that the Bank of England saved all Europe from bankruptcy, by furnishing them with 1,600,000l. ' It is a pity that a less sum than ten millions would not support the Emperor and his connections. Step in, Simon, and try if you can be of any use in putting the Bank of England in a way to save themselves.

It seems, from the original tenor of our constitution, that the landed interest of the country was placed as guardians over the property of the trading and lower classes of the people; but such hath been the conduct of the blind or lazy land-holder, the profits of the labour of industry is as much the estate of the opulent swindler, as the land is that encompasses their own mansions. It is to be hoped that this description of men will not always continue in a state of blindness, as it is certainly in their power to rescue the plundered multitude from a set of men whose moral characters were better calculated to be the keepers of E. O. Pharo, or any other game governed by private chicanery, than they were qualified as senators for an opulent trading nation.

Thursday December 22, in the House of Commons Mr. Pitt, agreeable to notice, rose to bring forward his bill for the relief of the poor. His plan did not differ from that which he proposed last year; it was his intention to have the bill committed before the recefs, in order that gentlemen might have an opportunity of confidering the meafure during that time; he then moved the introduction of the bill. Mr. Sheridan approved of the meafure, and hoped as Mr. Pitt had taken the plan out of the hands of an honourable gentleman (Mr. Whitbread) laft feffions, who would have expedited it, that the bill would not meet with any farther delay; the bill met his hearty concurrence, and he hoped the Houfe would adopt it. It is much to be feared, as Mr. Pitt hath been in the habit of making every thing worfe, that he will make no amendment by taking it out of the liberal hands that firft introduced it. Neceffary as an act of this kind muft appear, it is hoped no additional burthens will be levied on the handicraft tradefman, little fhopkeeper, or cottage publican; by all means let us wifh Mr. Pitt to avoid that kind of relief to the poor that he has produced in his extraordinary management of the public debt, which of courfe muft increafe their diftrefs, inftead of relieving them; as the money he hath wafted in that way is more than fufficient for ample provifion for all the poor in the kingdom for ever.

Mr. Paine's Downfal of the Englifh Funds.

Notwithftanding I am ready to acknowledge the abilities of Mr. Paine, as well as other eminent writers, on the fubject of finance, yet I have to declare that I have inveftigated none of thefe writers but have made fome principal errors in their calculations. For example; Mr. Paine fays that the proportion of time differs as much as from twenty to one as to the exiftence of credit, whether paper be payable on demand or funded. This muft certainly prove an error to every man that will inveftigate; for how can the funding of paper laft twenty times as long, when the rate of intereft of that paper has been continued at five and a half per cent. and the compound intereft will

will accumulate in such a way that not more than one in thirteen can be the difference? Again, it is impossible to draw any kind of average where a debt is so irregularly contracted; for example, Mr. Pitt hath contracted nearly as much new debt in three years as the average contracted before his time amounted to in threescore years; therefore, to a certainty, no probable line can be drawn that will ascertain the duration of the credit of this country on its present funding system. That new paper may be coined to any amount is certain, and from that circumstance no line can be drawn as to the length of the existence of national credit; and as the interest in the first instance produces hard cash, the existing credit will depend on the will and ability of the people to pay that interest, of which they seem so heartily sick, that I think it high time the potter's field was consecrated, that it might be ready to receive the innumerable herd of stock-jobbers and stock-brokers.

Again, Mr. Paine says the funded debt is four hundred millions, and the Bank notes sixty millions, and he supposes Mr. Pitt will fund them; in this Mr. Paine is also mistaken, for they are funded, and not now the debt of the public, but the debt of the Bank of England; and the public are by no means accountable for these notes, other than making good their payments of their funded securities; which if ever paid, it is most likely the Bank can pay their notes, amounting to at least eighty millions, without which it is impossible they can pay. For these notes no doubt but the Bank hath received funded securities, but who can estimate their value? However, it is a clear case that Government is not indebted to the public for the immense quantities of those notes in circulation, which is a circumstance every holder of a Bank-note ought to know. Again, Mr. Paine says before the war in 1755 there was no Bank notes lower than 20l. during that war Bank notes of 15l.

and of 10l. were issued, and now since the commencement of the present war, notes are issued so low as 5l. These 5l. notes will circulate chiefly amongst the little shopkeepers, butchers, bakers, market-people, renters of small houses, lodgers, &c. All the high departments of commerce, all the affluent stations in life, were already over-stocked (as Smith expresses it) with Bank-notes; but this was not the case amongst the class of people I have just mentioned, and the means of doing them service could be best effected by issuing 5l. notes. This conduct, Mr. Paine says, has the appearance of an unprincipled insolvent, who, when on the verge of bankruptcy to the amount of many thousands, will borrow as low as five pounds of the servants in his house, and break the next day; for whatever momentary relief or aid the Minister or his Bank may expect from this low contrivance of 5l. notes, it will increase the inability of the Bank to pay their higher notes, and hasten the destruction of all; for even such as used to be paid in money will now be paid in these small notes, and the Bank will soon find itself with scarcely any other money than what the hair-powder tax guinea brings in. Mr. Paine was also mistaken relative to the small notes shortening the existence of the Bank. On the contrary, it will lengthen the time of their existence, though the shock will be greater in the end. For the 5l. notes are in this way accommodating to the Bank, as without this contrivance, when the more opulent brought in their notes of 50l. and 20l. they must have been under the necessity of giving the value in cash; but in the present case three notes and 5l. in specie may answer the purpose.

The

The following is the extravagant ratio paid more by Englishmen to the revenue of their country than is paid by other subjects in the different states of Europe, as under.

1 Englishman pays as much as 6 Frenchmen did before the Revolution, perhaps as much as 10, at the conclusion of the peace.
1 Englishman as much as 12 in Turkey
1 ditto ——— 14 Russians
1 ditto ——— 10 Swedes
1 ditto ——— 3 Hollanders, *Stadtholdrian*
1 ditto ——— 6 Austrians
1 ditto ——— 5 Spaniards
1 ditto ——— 9 Portuguese

My countrymen justly complain that they find themselves heavily burthened, and, after all, seem at a loss how to state or identify their grievances. Therefore, in order to set them right in these important points, I shall state as under the difference in the prices of the necessaries of life within my own memory, that the most uninformed may know what they have to contend for.

Price of wheat, the Winchester bushel, between the years 1742 and 1748, 2s. 6d. now 9s. from the circumstance of Mr. Pitt's prohibiting, with the assistance of Lord Sheffield, the importation of foreign wheat, because it was no more than 6s. 8d. By this conduct the price hath been advanced from 5s. the Winchester bushel to 25s. This is proved in page 84, taken from Simon Pope's estimate in his letter to Citizen Curtis, late Lord Mayor of London. Mr. Pope is a principal advocate for Mr. Pitt.

Price

[104]

Price of Bread and other Necessaries of Life, from 1742 to 1748, with some little Variation.   *Present Price.*

Bread, 3d. the Quartern Loaf	0	0	8¼
Cheese, 2d. per lb.	0	0	8
Butter, 3d½	0	1	2
Beef 2d	0	0	8
Mutton 1d½	0	0	7
Lamb, 15d the Quarter	0	7	6
Veal, 1d½ per lb.	0	0	8
Pork, 2d	0	0	9
Bacon, 3d½	0	0	10
Turkey, 1s 6d*	0	7	6
Fat goose, 1s 2d*	0	6	0
Two ducks, 1s*	0	6	0
Two fowls, 8d*	0	6	0
Two ditto, half grown, 6d*	0	4	0
Sope, 3½	0	0	9
Candles, 4d	0	0	10
Barley, the Winchester bushel, 1s	0	4	6
Oats, ——— 8d	0	3	0
Oatmeal in proportion			
Malt, the Winchester bushel, 1s 6d	0	7	6
Rice, 1d¼ per lb.	0	0	3
Wine, at taverns, 1s 4d the bottle	0	3	6
French wines, that may be sold in England at 4d the bottle, and every cordial at the lowest mechanic's price.			
Prohibited brandy, the glass, 1d	0	0	4
——— rum, 1d	0	0	4
——— gin, ½d	0	0	2
Good amber ale, 2d½ the pot	0	0	6

The same quantity could then be brewed, by the cottager for one penny; at a time when he could afford to buy a brass kettle, and brew his own bushel

* These were the prices at country markets; of course some little expence must be added for bringing to Town.

of malt. Moſt of theſe laſt articles, ſays our heaven-born miniſter, are unbecoming the Swiniſh Multitude. And why? Becauſe Mr. Pitt hath more pride and impudence than is to be found again amongſt the human race. None of theſe bleſſings are prohibited by the all-bountiful Creator, but only by the wicked craft of our rulers.

On the 3,ſt of December, 1796, I was introduced to a reſpectable character who I found had been upon the continent to receive ſome property, and returned to this country the latter part of November; and from whom I learnt, that on his return through the French territory (towns ſuch as Thionville, Metz, Straſburg, &c. &c.) the following were the different prices of proviſions.

Beſt pieces of Pork   5d per lb. 18 oz.
Beef and Mutton   4
Veal — $3\frac{1}{2}$
Two Fowls   8

Wine at the inns at the extravagant price of 8d. the bottle, on account of the failures of ſeveral of the vintages; but not ſo dear, by more than one half the difference, in other parts of the country, where the crops were more productive.

Coffee — 2s per lb. 18 oz.
Butter — 6d
Bacon — $6\frac{1}{2}$

All theſe articles dearer now than before the war.

Price of wheat 15s the ſack, containing four Wincheſter buſhels, at 3s 9d

This article is now importing at the rate of 13s. the Wincheſter buſhel, according to Simon Pope's account, who ſays, that our virtuous Adminiſtration has been ranſacking all the granaries in the world to procure it; and it comes home to the conſumer at no leſs a price than 25s the Wincheſter buſhel, as Mr. Pitt is in the habit of paying two for one for the loan of the money to pay for this grain, the amount being

being upwards of two millions: and whether it be raised by a tax on the article, or on any thing else, the effect is the same to the country in the end.

Price of Hay 15d the cwt. or 25s the ton.
Oats 7s 6d the sack, containing four Winchester bushels, at 1s 10½d
Beans, two sacks, 10s 6d eight Winchester bushels, is 3¾d the bushel

Expences for a man and horse for one night at an inn for the following accommodations—a fowl for supper, a pint of wine, coffee for breakfast, hay and two feeds of corn for the horse—total expence 2s 4d

I wish my deluded countrymen to read and consider which Mr. Pitt is likely to starve first, the French or the English. But alas! such is the credulity of Englishmen, that they will sing a song about the roast beef of Old England, though they never taste it but once in seven years, and that at an election.

A most serious topic, to fulfil my engagement to the public, is the five hundred million funded debt. How Mr. Pitt hath borrowed two hundred millions in the last three years, in a country that doth not possess more than ten millions that can possibly come into public use, is the most paradoxical business we shall ever hear of. Surely the black art must have been at work in Downing-street or Holwood House. He must have engaged Devils and Doctor Fosters in abundance. I think I could guess at a few of these demons that have had long fingers in the pie— Right Honourable Harry Scott, Earl of Shark Pool, with my Lord Green Park. Is not suspicion asleep? Is not Opposition asleep? Have not my countrymen nodded away their reason to the wink of the heaven-born minister? After all, how can it be possible that Mr. Pitt can have borrowed two hundred millions in a country that does not contain more than ten millions at any one time for the public service, nor nearly so much? But give me the hammer,
and

and I'll hit the right nail on the head. Ye virtuous and moſt penetrating Oppoſition, call upon the directors of the Bank of England to produce an account of the amount of their outſtanding notes; then we can come to a certainty as to the ſums paid by the induſtrious part of the country for the loan of paper, to theſe liberal feeds of Shylock, theſe uncircumciſed Jews.

Peace being ſo confiſtent with the object of œconomical finance, I find myſelf under the neceſſity of introducing it a ſecond time. Every liberal minded Engliſhman cannot have forgot, that twenty-ſeven millions of Frenchmen and good ſoldiers were humiliating enough to have continued in peace, and that the war was and is Mr. Pitt's darling object; and he will continue it as long as he poſſibly can.—Was it the intention of Brunſwick to level the city of Paris with a view of rebuilding it? or was it to cauſe diſtreſs, and the deſolation of that city?—If the latter, is it not found policy in the governors of Paris to keep to the extent of their ramparts, to ſave their city from deſtruction? Why then is Mr. Pitt to expect that the Netherlands will be given up to the Emperor?—No: Mr. Pitt does not expect it. The object of peace I conſider to be at his will; and that it will be left till he thinks he has ſufficient ſtrength to cut up his injured countrymen. Quere—May not Billy be miſtaken?—No doubt but he thinks that there will be no difficulty in ſetting twenty thouſand young heroes on horſeback, who will be more likely to have their grandmothers to fight againſt for grumbling about taxes, or quite children crying for the want of bread, than an invading foe. But in the mean time may it be remembered, that twenty thouſand horſes will require as much land to ſupport them as would find one hundred thouſand poor children with every neceſſary of life. But as the money is ſo nearly exhauſted, and ſoldiers and ſailors muſt

be

be paid with guineas, I wifh fome honourable gentleman would afk Mr. Pitt what he intends to do with thefe men.—Is it his intention to offer them as prefents to the nobility, for cultivating their lands? Certainly the poor men ought to know what they have to expect.

A fair queftion—Mr. Pitt, was Lord Malmfbury fent to Paris with a view to obtain a peace? or was it in order to raife fupplies to carry on the war?

———

Now for my New Syftem of Finance and Compromife, though I think that fome hundreds that ftand in the lift of creditors deferve a halter as the beft recompence: but it is a pity that the innocent fhould fuffer for the guilty. My views are, to have the dreadful cataftrophe avoided that hath attended a neighbouring nation, and fecure the property of the widow and fatherlefs; to find the means of bringing the neceffaries of life to the induftrious part of the community on reafonable terms, and to avoid a degree of refentment that may be equal to madnefs; to prevent the maffacre of the inhuman plunderers of their country, as innocent victims may fall with them, and to eftablifh public credit as firm as the Perfian laws, that cannot alter. But I am confident that no fubftantial root of reform can take place without a change in the Adminiftration of our country, and a peace eftablifhment: and when that is happily effected, the following is my plan for the New Syftem of Finance.

The firft material object will be, the eftablifhment of National Banks. And in order to avoid as much as poffible any check on the trade of the country that it may be fubject to, let an account be delivered into a well collected Adminiftration of all the Bank-notes now

now in circulation, and an equal number and value be coined. Let the new notes be headed with the king's head, or any other conspicuous figure, so that the most illiterate holder of a bank-note may at first sight discover the difference; and let the same now nominal Bank of England notes be brought into the public treasury, and exchanged for new notes of equal number and value; and as they come in, pay the said bank in their own coin, and take up the securities they now hold of every description in the public funds. This, supposing them to be no more than about eighty millions, will produce annual savings to the amount of — 4,000,000

Profits of the banks throughout the kingdom, on a very low computation — — 1,500,000

Sums paid annually to the Bank for management ——— 300,000

Five hundred millions in the 3 per cents. reduced to 50l. which is about the proportion of what the minister is now borrowing, and pay 4 per cent. interest, which will produce annual savings to the amount of ——— 5,000,000

10,800,000

But as the saving cannot operate in both cases, relative to the securities cancelled by the Bank, it is necessary to deduct one-third from the above 4,000,000l.   1,333,333 6 8

9,466,666 13 4

Add to this, profits on the funds for the benefit of age
Benefits of all other legal societies

Total

Total amount of savings brought forward ———   9,466,666 13 4

Benefits arising from the turn-pikes throughout the kingdom, calculating 100l. profit on every gate, will bring a profit of   500,000 0 0

It will be useful for the governors to take every description of idle money into this treasury

9,966,666 13 4

A few years since an additional charge took place on the toll gates at Bath, to the amount of fifty per cent. when it must appear to be almost impossible fairly to spend the former income. From interest of money and expence of repairing, with the above proposed alteration in the funds, I imagine there will be much quirking by and by for the monied men. I answer, that there are no such objects in existence as monied men, if you deal fairly by the people, and they will act wisely for themselves. There being no more than fifteen millions in the kingdom, and not more than ten millions to be spared for public use, it is but fair to explain to whom it belongs. The manufacturer that sells his woollen or linen cloths, manufacturers of gold and silver, and metals of every description; the farmer for hay, corn, and cattle; the shopkeeper, taylor, shoemaker, publican, and every handicraft tradesman, give solid value, and turn two or three times in the year the value of the whole of the specie, and certainly can demand cash in the stead of bank-notes, which they are now glad to receive: of course the Bank of England drains all the cash; and as a liberal return look at Mr. Pitt's contract for money and paper with that virtuous company. A most convincing proof—witness the Emperor's loan. Mr. Pitt obtained 4 1l. 10 s.

10s. 8d. and for every such sum he bound this country to pay 100l. in the 3 per cents. I would wish to ask the industrious part of my countrymen whether they can possibly continue so blind as to give a preference to that paper nick-named the Bank of England paper, as the country is no more bound to make good any deficiency that may accrue to the Bank from the misconduct of its directors, than they would be from the failure of a bank in Jerusalem: therefore it is not the Bank of England, but a Bank in England, supported in the most extravagant degree of usury and extortion at the expence of the public. No doubt but I shall be told by the director, stock-jobber, &c. that the present bank is the best security for money; as for example, they have been always punctual in their payments: and no doubt they will continue so, as long as they can find an annual profit of 40 per cent. on their capital; for in fact it is more their interest to continue punctual in their payments than it would be to run away with the capital. As to the bank I have been speaking of, it is impossible it can be an additional security to the public creditor, but on the contrary an additional risque; for if the directors of this bank do not in the first instance receive from the exchequer, it is impossible they can pay; and if they do receive, it is possible they may not pay. And I would ask my countrymen to which they would give the preference as a private security for their thousand or their ten thousand, that on an estate burthened with a heavy annuity, or that on one nearly free? Of course they would take to that estate that had the least incumbrance. And if this be prudence in a private transaction, it must be so in a public one. And are not the savings so conspicuous in this New System and Reform, as to prove it an object worth the attention of every thinking man of property, or a man barely in existence by means of his own industry. It is a
clear

clear cafe, that by taking paper you give your money to the bank; and as a public debtor you put the means of ufury and extortion into the power of thefe people; by which reafon you are compelled to pay extravagantly for the ufe of your own money, It is like putting a piftol into the hands of a highwayman to blow your brains out.

My motive for laying thefe facts before you is, that you may fee the utility of that part of my new Syftem of Finance, by your giving a preference to national banks. And have you not, as another inftance, a recent proof of the happy confequences of public banks? Governor Mifflin, in his declaration to the Affembly at Pennfylvania, ftates that the profits of their bank are more than fufficient to pay the expences of the ftate: from the intereft of their money alone, they have a furplus to make public canals and to repair the public roads.

It is but now I hear the principal obftacle to a peace, which is, that the French refufe to give back to the Emperor the Netherlands. Should we not act in our public capacity the fame difinterefted part as we would in a private capacity—do as we would be done by? Do we not hold from the French the iflands of Guernfey, Jerfey, Alderney, and Sark, for the very fame reafon—as a prevention of the annoyance of our coaft? And have not the French the fame reafon to wifh to hold the Netherlands, as a fafeguard for the city of Paris? Did not the Duke of Brunfwick threaten and attempt to enter Paris with an army, and with a view to deftroy it, and make a facrifice to his ambition of every foul in that populous city? Therefore how can fuch caution be thought extravagant or unreafonable, and which is fo exactly fimilar to the part we have been acting ourfelves relative to the neighbouring iflands? Do not our rulers know, that an application to a fuccefsful antagonift would bid fairer for fuccefs through any other channel than

from

from Mr. Pitt, a man juftly detefted by every nation in Europe; a man, as the Tu ks fay, that hath been embroiling all t e nations in Europe, in order to profit by his perfidy. And when can we be better convinced of this fact, than when we find we are deftitute of every powerful ally except the Emperor, who ftill continues kindly to falute the Fnglifh guineas, of which he is now in poffeffion of at leaft twenty waggon loads. Peace is the grand object with every rational man, who muft think the greater the diftance the terms will be the worfe, and that better terms may be made with France through any other channel than the ftarving Mr. Pitt.

Amount of annual favings from New Syftem of Finance, brought over £.0, 66 696 13 4

From this e traordinary faving the following taxes may be annihilated with the ftricteft juftice to debtor and creditor, and the people find almoft immediate relief. The duties may ceafe on malt, hops, wine, fpirits, and cordials of every defcription; falt, foap, candles, leather, and every other article in common confumption with the poor: and with a peace eftablifhment a handfome furplus will remain for the purpofe of difcharging the debt, efpecially if a free intercourfe of trade fhould take place between the two nations, freed from the burthen of taxes.

After eafing the people from the above, the numerous taxes remaining will be found to anfwer every reafonable purpofe, though perhaps not to gratify the opulent and avaricious fwindler. If circumftances fhould happen to require a more than common demand, what can be done better than adding a per centage to fuch of the taxes as fhall appear the leaft burthenfome?

It is a clear cafe, that the abundant produce of the vines in France will produce a furplus fufficient, in a plentiful year to fupply this country fo, as that the publican may be able to fell at the very low price of

I 4d.

4d. the bottle, as Camus lately declared in the Affembly of Five Hundred, that in a plentiful year they made as much wine as could be confumed by eighty millions of people, and that it was worth no more than two fous the pint, which is equal to an Englifh penny.

This change taken place, our Englifh ale and beer may be brought to the old ftandard—a quality fcarcely known at the prefent period. In that cafe, no doubt but many would prefer their own country beverage to French wines. But ftill we have to confider the aftonifhing difference from the numbers that would drink the French wines, what an influx of grain it would bring to our markets, on account of the reduced confumption of wheat and barley in our brewhoufes and diftilleries; we fhall have occafion for a fmaller quantity of tillage land, and of courfe be able to multiply the quantity of animal food of every defcription: and can our rulers be fo ignorant as not to fee that we could with more cheerfulnefs fupport them in fplendor?

Another proof of the neceffity of our endeavours to increafe the quantity of provifions— The beginning of December a woman was found dead in the road near Birmingham; as were alfo a man and woman, in each other's arms, near Petticoat-lane, London; all died for the want of the neceffaries of life. And can we doubt of numbers now languifhing in the fame fituation?—As all thefe dreadful cataftrophes do not affect the feelings of our Adminiftration, can there be a doubt of the neceffity of a change?

There can be no doubt but that the loweft rate of our woollen manufactories will be readily received in France as a barter for their wines, and the idea of fmuggling our wool into France be done away. The manufacture of finer goods, fuch as broad cloth, kerfeymere, &c. we may fuppofe to be as well done

in

in France as in England, as they have with us an equal or better chance for the Spanish wool.

Let us endeavour to do away the prejudice of education. It has been the practice of our rulers to sow discord between the two nations: and this they have done by representing the French as the most deceitful, poor, beggarly people in Europe, or the world, destitute of the means of any tolerable existence; that the whole course of their lives was starving poverty: and we were persuaded to treat them as though they were created for the contempt of the human race. What foundation could my countrymen have to credit this kind of information, when nothing was more common than for these same people who gave this kind of information, to go and spend their money in a country they so much despised? Why was this crafty deception carried on, but to deprive the lower orders of the people of the advantages that naturally must have accrued from a friendly intercourse between the two nations; and with no other advantages to themselves, than the pride of the most extravagant distinction between man and man? But we are now convinced that the very reverse of what we have been made to believe is the fact; that there is not a finer garden in Europe than France; that they abound with corn and wine —with almost every necessary for the comfortable support of the human race; and, notwithstanding their late devastations, it is in their power to supply this country with every necessary of life that we stand in need of. That they are liberal is allowed by their enemies; and they are ready to take their insulting foe by the hand, as soon as they shall appear to have received a sense of their own interest. It is not only humanity, but our interest, calls aloud for peace, and a friendly intercourse with France. But how is this great object to be obtained? We cannot be assisted by our overgrown, rich rulers, who profit so much by carnage; nor does there appear sincerity enough in Opposition to give any staple support to the cause. We are told of a Whig Club, men of fortune and ability: But what do they do?—They meet at the Crown and Anchor—eat a good dinner—have constitutional toasts—drink the bottles, one, two, three, huzza! and mellow or sober, go to bed, Tom; and thus ends their patriotism.'

If Opposition had been sincere, would they not have brought the minister to account, to prove what had been received for two hundred millions; and the Bank of England, to prove what they had advanced for the immense securities which they held against the public? Do these pretended advocates for reform ever think of the unfortunate victims confined now in the dreary prisons, for distinguished manliness in their opposition to our persecuting, ruling plunderers of their country? Nor did they come forward in behalf of those few noble patriots that risqued the trials for their lives for the cause, who are now no more thought of than if such men had never been in existence. At the same time they appear ready to spend their thousands and tens of thousands to support a party, lest we mistake ourselves as to that description of men that are the supporters of this most accursed war. I wish to explain to my readers, that it is all the powerful side of the House of Commons; every man in opposition that voted for the supplies to carry on the war; all the monied men, paper men, and swindling stock-jobbers, out of the House; in fact, every man that holds a 5l. bank-note for a day only, is a supporter of this cursed war, without which it could not be carried on.

I wish to call the attention of my countrymen to that unfortunate victim of ministerial vengeance, Citizen Smith, condemned by Judge Ashhurst for the sin of his mother. The old gentlewoman sold a book.

book. But could the crime be brought home to Mr Smith? If it should be his fate to be condemned to the Clerkenwell Baſtille for two years, his fate will be more deplorable than that of the unfortunate Burks. Mr. Smith being of a weak conſtitution, this Baſtille muſt ſoon be his grave; and Mrs. Smith be an unfortunate widow, with four or five, I do not know which, helpleſs children, unprovided for. It is therefore hoped, that the liberal citizen, the Samaritan, going by with two-pence in his pocket that he can ſpare, will call at No. 1, Portſmouth-ſtreet, Lincoln's Inn Fields, and buy a book of the poor widow.

Commercial Bank—Commercial Swindle! or laſt Shoe in the Miniſter's Shop.

Mr. Pitt's plan for raiſing two millions ſterling, for the accommodation of trade. He propoſes for a company of merchants to join and coin notes to the amount of two millions; that perſons having title deeds, mortgage deeds, navy, victualling, tranſport, and exchequer bills, funded ſecurities, which he calls ſolid property, lodging theſe ſecurities in the ſaid bank, ſhall be liable to receive thoſe notes in lieu of their ſecurities, and the public be compelled to take them as caſh for the ſpace of two years; for which the receivers of theſe notes from the bank are liable to pay an intereſt of five per cent. So that if people will be ſuch dupes, they are to lodge ſolid ſecurities in exchange for what is not ſolid property. Mr. Pitt brings two millions more paper into circulating medium: But, inſtead of the aid of trade, can any man be ſo blind as not to ſee that Mr. Pitt's views are, to bring this circulating medium to ſtock funding? And as this ſum, if he has the whole, will not furniſh him with a month's expences, where will this new bank find money at the end of two years to take up their notes?

In

Prior to the year 1788, I addressed a letter to Mr. Pitt to secure for the benefit of the public the money that was wasted by the adventurers in lotteries.

The following was my plan. That as the profits to the dealers in lottery tickets did not average less than fifty per cent. the money wasted by this extravagant folly might be saved to the adventurers partly in their taxes. I recommended to Government to issue out tickets at 13l. each, and advance in their regular progression to the time of drawing; and the venders of tickets be allowed a commission equal to the custom of selling stamps. By this mode I proved, that Government might get at least 200,000l. by every lottery, and the adventurers go to market in pursuit of their prizes on rather better terms than before the alteration took place. By this recommendation Mr. Pitt saw clearly that a profit was easily secured to Government on the sale of state lottery tickets, which prior to that time seldom went off without a bonus to the subscribers. Mr. Pitt, consistent with his general practice of concealing the channel from which he has obtained any useful information, puts the tickets up to the hammer, and they were the first year knocked down to the highest bidder, with a profit to Government of two hundred thousand pounds, which hath been pretty generally the case with every lottery since. But laying no restraint, as I recommended, on the price of the tickets, they operated as a stock-jobbing article, and the alteration proved an additional tax of forty per cent. to the adventurers; the former price being from 13 to 15l. the ticket, and since Mr. Pitt's alteration from 17 to 20l. though that cannot be the case for the present year, as the original value of the ticket is reduced to the amount of 1l. 13s. 4d. of course a 10l. ticket is this year worth no more than 8l. 6s. 8d.

Mr.

Mr. Pitt is certainly in want of yellow-boys, gold-finches, or something that will anfwer the purpofe of money. The great number of defaulters in the laft loan, and the Bank being tired of coining paper, muft be fufficient proofs of it. I have been in one inftance ferviceable to the minifter; but I do not fee that I lie under any obligation to do the like again, as he took care to conceal the channel through which he procured his information. But, however, let me confider the credit of my country as being at the laft ftake, and, giving up perfonal refentment for public utility, advife him a fecond time.—Let there be expreffes fent round the kingdom to every farm-houfe, with particular orders to fave their hens' eggs, and another exprefs to Germany for Herman Boaz; and he will undertake, with his magic hammer and ufual dexterity, to knock out a goldfinch from every one of thofe eggs. And furely there cannot be a more fuitable fupply; as during the continuance of Mr. Pitt's adminiftration money muft fly in and out of the treafury, and a goldfinch is certainly a more folid fecurity than a fcrip of paper.

Since writing the above, I hear the loyalty loan has dropped 6 per cent. Shocking times indeed!— Will not Brandon the trufs-maker fay, " It's a bad wind that blows nobody good: I'll go down to the Stock Exchange before the doors are open, and pick up plenty of orders for binding up the lame ducks?"

But to be more ferious in this important bufinefs. There is certainly no nation in Europe, whofe credit has been drawn into fo much ridicule and contempt as this country's has been in Mr. Pitt's adminiftration, particularly during the laft three years. Eight millions of fpecie is certainly all that could be appropriated for the public ufe at any one time. The loan-mongers muft have turned it twenty-five times in the fhort period of the laft three years, or made up the

deficiency

deficiency in paper. The fact is, that as soon as Mr. Pitt hath finished his funding for the present outstanding debts, the loan-monger's eight millions must increase to two hundred millions, twenty-five times the sum they first started upon.

Such a degree of extravagance, of public sacrifice of public property, surely never could have entered the brain of any other than our heaven born minister. And in all this time the country is not a shilling the richer, but ten millions the poorer, having sent so much out of the country as foreign subsidies. How then are the loan-mongers to be satisfied for this astonishing sum, but from new mortgages on the labours of the people, from whom they are in hopes to receive their extravagant interest? Is not the Administration as ignorant as wicked, to suppose that ever such unreasonable contracts can be completed?

After all, it is but fair to give some idea of the loyalty and ability of some of our opulent bodies politic. The city of London have offered to lend Government one hundred thousand pounds, if they can tell where to borrow it: the India Company, two millions, if they can raise 3,40,000l. on their new created stock. But all these, if attended with success, are but contemptible trifles towards the support of the continuance of the minister's wicked measures; and every man of humanity must rejoice to see that they are so near at an end, from whatever cause it may proceed. We never can say we have been sincere in an offer to make peace with the French through the channel of Mr. Pitt; for if it comes through him, they know it is from necessity. In all private concerns, if we want to make friendship with any man, we make choice of the person that we think would be the most palatable to his temper: and we know, for very just reasons, there cannot be a man more detested by the French than Mr. Pitt must be.

In

In my account of East India produce, I omitted the article of sugar, so much in consumption. Price in the country, retailed at two-pence half-penny the pound, could not cost the company more than twenty-one shillings the hundred weight; freight and insurance home seven shillings: delivered into the company's warehouses at three-pence the pound. Another proof, that nothing can be obtained at a moderate price through the hands of a monopolizing company.

Now, my fellow citizens, if you read this treatise attentively, you will see the cause of your present deplorable situation, and the means of relief; that it entirely depends on the efforts of you that are persecuted. Your numbers will prove you to be the support of the nation—the strength of the nation. But be unanimous, discreet, and manly in your operations. More than thirty years experience proves that petitioning is vain; therefore you must remonstrate.

It is not the sparing hand of Providence that hath distressed us, for we experience his liberality in our own corn fields; and our situation with other countries for other necessaries of life, are proofs of it. It is our rulers that lay restraints on his bounty. Let us therefore endeavour to open the eyes of the King. —Though I will not pretend to dictate a remonstrance to you, yet I shall take the liberty of stating some important objects that I think will strengthen your cause for complaint.

May it please your Majesty to consider, that we know it is in the power of the King to find relief for his distressed subjects; and we believe it to be your interest to do so. The whole of your Majesty's reign has been unfortunate for yourself, and more so for your afflicted subjects, from the circumstance of your having employed, we believe, the most wicked in this kingdom in your administration. While they have been

K

been ringing a deceitful peal in your Majesty's ears, advising you to fight for religion, they have been indulging themselves as the most extravagant wine bibbers, friends to tax-gatherers and sinners only, with the addition of every other luxury and licentiousness; in fact, they appear to be affected like wild asses in the morning, every man neighing after his neighbour's wife. Of this fact Doctor's Commons bears record.

This is their situation, while the more industrious part of your Majesty's subjects are strangers to every degree of happiness, nor know one day how to provide the taxes for the next; and the very lowest orders of the people dying for the want of the necessaries of life. It is no stranger than true, that such has been the increase of the burthens during your Majesty's reign, that it is as much as four to one; and we find that by comparing our situation with that of other European nations, though mixed with the most barbarous states of despotism, yet is our incumbrance as much as eight to one. So that we have more taxes to provide for in one day than all the inhabitants in Europe besides ourselves have to provide for in a week.

In the midst of all this, your Majesty's ministers have the impudence to tell us, that we live too well. Not confining themselves to the spilling of human blood, and taxation, they have summoned all their arts to increase the price of the necessaries of life, by prohibiting the importation of grain in particular, whenever it was to be obtained in the country on moderate terms.

The public credit we conceive to be an object of your Majesty's most serious consideration, as we imagine that part of your Majesty's fortune that is fixed in this kingdom is settled in the public funds; and any encroachment to lessen its credit must be injurious to your Majesty. Mr. Pitt hath added two hundred millions

millions to the public debt, in the proportion of three per cent. principally during the laſt three years, and for which very little money hath been received; though it is an additional annual charge, it is not any increaſe of national wealth, but additional mortgage on the labours of the people. This certainly has brought on an inſolvent ſecurity, as it is impoſſible the people can pay And it is the more provoking, as very little ſolid property can have been received for this immenſe ſum; it being a well known faƈt, that the ſpecie in the kingdom for public uſe does not amount to a twentieth part of the ſum ſpent by Mr. Pitt. But as long as we do exiſt in credit, the labours of the people are ſwindled into the hands of the ſtock jobber to the amount of two hundred millions, principally from the circumſtance of ſhuffling paper from hand to hand.

This being really the caſe, it is humbly hoped your Majeſty will ſee the neceſſity and utility of a peace with France, a general intercourſe of trade, unincum ered with taxes, a compromiſe between debtor and creditor, the people eaſed of their taxes, a circumſtance eaſily obtained, and will be the cauſe of the neceſſaries of life being an eaſy acquiſition to all the induſtrious part of your Majeſty's ſubjeƈts.

My advice to you, my countrymen, is, that you meet in your lawful aſſemblies, and that the moſt ſenſible amongſt you draw up a reaſonable remonſtrance to the King. Let it be ſigned in all your diviſions, and there can be no doubt but your example will be followed by the perſecuted inhabitants in every borough and city in the kingdom.

I have now only to add, that in this important buſineſs I recommend you to be unanimous, ſteady, and manly; a conduct which I think will be the means of crowning your endeavours with ſucceſs in this moſt important undertaking.

In

In America, a widow, with four or five children is courted as a fortune, the labour of every child being worth 1col.—in England a situation the most wretched. Why?—Because the neceſſaries of life are ſo frequently prohibited, or loaded with heavy duties.

We may be told by ſuch as wiſh to ſupport the preſent exorbitant prices of the neceſſaries of life, that the price of labour is advanced in proportion. But that I deny: ſome addition has indeed taken place in the metropolis and its neighbourhood, but that by no means in proportion to the extravagant price of proviſions. It is within a very ſhort period, that I have ſeen able-bodied men working in the two counties of Hereford and Glouceſter, in the fields, at ten pence per day, and in Wales at eight pence: if there has been any advance in Devonſhire, it is not more than two pence per day to the huſbandman. A recent application by petition was made by this very uſeful ſet of men: they were anſwered, at a meeting at the Caſtle at Exeter, that that was no time to raiſe wages; but never gave them the ſatisfaction to ſay, that it was becauſe Mr. Pitt was ſpending ſo much of the public money. Some of the poor woollen manufacturers, who are numerous, get leſs money now than they did when the price of the neceſſaries of life were at the loweſt I have mentioned.

www.ingramcontent.com/pod-product-compliance
Lightning Source LLC
Chambersburg PA
CBHW020110170426
43199CB00009B/480